Property of
Charles A. Owen, Jr.
Medieval Studies Library

HISTORY OF BANSTEAD IN SURREY

BY

Sir HENRY C. M. LAMBERT
K.C.M.G., C.B.

Property of
Charles A. Owen, Jr.
Medieval Studies Library

VOLUME II

OXFORD UNIVERSITY PRESS
LONDON : HUMPHREY MILFORD
1931

DA690.B225.L3 vol.2 1931

OXFORD UNIVERSITY PRESS
AMEN HOUSE, E.C. 4
LONDON EDINBURGH GLASGOW
LEIPZIG NEW YORK TORONTO
MELBOURNE CAPETOWN BOMBAY
CALCUTTA MADRAS SHANGHAI
HUMPHREY MILFORD
PUBLISHER TO THE
UNIVERSITY

PRINTED IN GREAT BRITAIN

PREFACE

THE first volume of this book, which appeared in 1912, gave (as no one realized more thoroughly than the author) a very incomplete history of the parish, and the present volume is an attempt to supply some of the omissions. It contains some corrections and results of reconsideration, some material which has already appeared in different volumes of the Surrey Archaeological Collections, or in a little volume of lectures given in 1923,[1] which it seemed worth while to bring together, and some entirely new material. It still leaves far more ground uncovered than it attempts to cover, but since to write the complete history of any parish is impossible, it seemed better to concentrate on such parts as from the relative abundance of the material or the capacity (or deficiencies) of the investigator seemed to promise the best results. In particular a much more thorough examination of the information to be obtained from the medieval Court Rolls has been made.

The plan followed in the first volume of printing original documents has been adhered to, except that to avoid expense Latin documents have been extended without indicating the precise contraction on which the extension is based. In particular a number of extracts from Court Rolls have been printed. Court Rolls are so bulky and contain so much repetition that it is impossible to present them except in extract or summary, and it has been by no means easy to decide what extracts to print. The plan adopted has been to print a number of Courts, each complete in itself, and selected either because it seemed typical or because it had some special point of interest, e.g. the Court of 4 November 1378 is the earliest Court with View extant and that of 29 July 1433 is the last Court before the Banstead Roll is lost for half a century. One Court is given when the roll resumes in the reign of Henry VII, one instance

[1] Banstead: three lectures on its history. Simpkin, Marshall. Hamilton, Kent, & Co., Ltd. [1924].

for the reign of Henry VIII, and one for Elizabeth. But it must be admitted that another selection might have been made. The extracts printed will in any case give a good idea of the forms used and the nature of the business transacted, and it is hoped that they may be of use to others engaged in similar studies in other parishes. The Tadworth Rolls fortunately supply some material for that part of the fifteenth century for which the Banstead Roll is missing. The Banstead Court Rolls have been easy to consult, having been lodged at the Public Record Office by the courtesy of the Steward of the Manor. I am indebted to Mr. Gerald Russell for allowing me to examine the Tadworth Court Roll. To the Council of the Surrey Archaeological Society I am obliged for permission to use material including some of the illustrations (I, IV, V, and VI) published in their collections. I have to thank Mr. Giuseppi and Mr. Jenkinson of the Record Office for help on various points.

It was observed in the first volume that there had been, until quite recently, no considerable amount of building in the parish to obliterate old landmarks. These words are no longer true, and Banstead has not been exempt since the War from those influences which are ruining the face of England. This book, however, is concerned with the past, not with the present or the future, and I will only add that while no one can study the past in detail and attempt to understand what it really was without seeing how great, and indeed in some respects how glaring, its defects were, it still remains true that former generations had in one respect a great advantage over us. They lived in a world which was unquestionably more beautiful than our own, and one which will probably seem more and more so in comparison with anything that our successors can hope to see. Plate II illustrates the kind of thing which has disappeared, to be replaced by something else which may be more convenient, but has less beauty and less character.

CONTENTS

APPENDIX OF DOCUMENTS

ILLUSTRATIONS

ABBREVIATIONS

C. P. R. Calendars of the Patent Rolls preserved in the Public Record Office.

D. N. B. Dictionary of National Biography.

H. M. C. Historical Manuscripts Commission.

J. Giles Jacob, Law Dictionary (ed. of 1809).

M. B. Manning and Bray, History of Surrey (1804–14).

N. E. D. A New English Dictionary on historical principles (the Oxford Dictionary).

R. O. Public Record Office.

S. A. C. Surrey Archaeological Collections from 1858.

V. H. S. The Victoria History of the County of Surrey.

NOTE.—All dates are given according to modern style—thus 17 March, 3 Edward VI, the regnal year beginning in January, is given as 1549, not 1548.

I

THE MANOR OF BANSTEAD CUM MEMBRIS

'THE Manor of Bansted', say Manning and Bray, 'is stiled, *Bansted cum membris*. It extends into *Leigh* and *Horley*, in the *Weald*, and at the Court Baron there are two homages sworn, one for the upper part, *Bansted*, the other for the *Weald*. At the Court Leet a constable is chosen for *Bansted* and another for *Tadworth*. Tithingmen for *Bansted* are called *primus, secundus, tertius*, sometimes *quartus*, and there are tithingmen for *Tadworth, Copthill, Chaldon, Dunshett* (in *Leigh*), *Sidlow-mill* and *Wallington*; an aletaster for *Bansted*.'[1]

How these outlying parts of the manor came to be acquired it is impossible to say. There is no sign of them in Domesday Book, but they appear long before the earliest extant Court Roll.[2]

Alnod held Banstead in the time of Edward the Confessor and Richard of Tonbridge held it of Odo, Bishop of Bayeux, at the time of the Domesday Survey,[3] which also shows certain subinfeudations.

The next known possessor was Tirel de Maniers, who in the time of Henry I gave the Church of Benestede to the Priory of St. Mary Overee at Southwark, a Convent of Augustinian Canons, whose church is now Southwark Cathedral. From him the manor descended to William FitzPatrick by marriage with his daughter Eleanor, and he gave it with his daughter Mabel to Nigel de Mowbray. Nigel together with Mabel his wife confirmed the grant of the church. After the death of Nigel, when

[1] M. B. ii. 582 (1809). In the British Museum are some maps of the manor (Add. MS. 36307, 4 and 5) undated but apparently about that date. They are in a miscellaneous collection of maps, but beyond that they were given to the Museum by Mr. D. H. Barry in 1890, nothing seems known of their origin. The map of the manor below the hill includes Beer or Buries, Wolvers, Rayes*, Crutfield*, Whyatts, Hutchings, Dean Farm, the Axes*, Watts*, Strutfield, Tapners, Minchingfield*, Fetheridge*, and Tanyard*. Those marked * are coloured blue and the rest yellow, the blue being apparently the copyhold.

[2] See the list of tenants in the Weald in the Extent of 1325, which also refers to Chaldon. The Court Roll begins in 1378. For the tithings at that time see p. 18.

[3] i. 28.

he also gave the church of Berges (Borough) to the Priory, the manor descended to his son William de Mowbray.[1]

This William was one of the Barons who were in arms with Louis of France against Henry III and was captured in May 1217 at Lincoln. It is alleged by Manning and Bray that his lands were seized, and that Hubert de Burgh having procured their restoration, he gave to Hubert the Manor of Banstead. It is, however, stated by Matthew Paris that no fines or confiscations were inflicted when peace was made and the manor may have passed to Hubert by purchase.[2] Hubert's tenure of Banstead was endangered by his political troubles,[3] and he seems at one time to have mortgaged it to the Templars.[4] He retained possession, however, at his death, which occurred at his Manor of Banstede.[5] He was buried in London. His house, according to a tradition preserved by Aubrey[6] and confirmed by other evidence, was at the east end of Banstead church yard where there was a pit, said to be the remains of the cellars.

His widow Margaret, sister of Alexander King of Scotland, after some trouble[7] was confirmed in her holding of the manor. The Inquisition taken on her death in 1258[8] shows that she held the Manor of Roger de Munbray for three knights' fees[9] and he held of the King in Chief. John de Burk, a son of Hubert by an earlier marriage, was next heir. John, who was Constable of the Tower of London, conveyed the manor to Edward I,[10] and it

[1] See M. B. ii. 582, and the Charters printed in Dugdale's Monasticon, vi. 171 (ed. 1830).

[2] Paris, Chron. Maj. iv. 31. See Feet of Fines, Surrey, Easter, 11 Henry III, No. 78, by which Nigel de Mowbray after his father's death quitclaimed the manor to Hubert and his wife Margaret and their heirs in fee by the service of three knights for all service (1227).

[3] See Close Roll (Henry III), 13 Nov. 1232, and Paris, Hist. Angl. ii. 351.

[4] Close Roll, 7 Feb. 1233.

[5] M. Paris, Hist. Angl. ii. 477.

[6] See i. 218.

[7] Close Roll, 27 Henry III, Part II.

[8] Printed in Appendix.

[9] It appears from the Testa de Nevill that William Hansard had held two knights' fees in Taddewurth of the Earl of Kent (Hubert de Burgh) of the Honour of Munbray, and John de Bures one in Berewe of the same.

[10] C. P. R. 16 Dec. 1273. The King's title to the manor did not, apparently, become complete till 1275, when William de Apeltrefeud, to whom John de Burgh had alienated the manor without licence in 1272, remitted and quitclaimed his right in the manor, the King pardoning him 1,000 marks in which he was bound in the King's Jewry (Calendar of Close Rolls, 22 May 1275).

remained a royal manor, generally forming part of the dowry of the queens of England till the time of Henry VIII.

In 1275 the manor was granted by Edward I together with other lands to his Queen, Eleanor of Castile, for the purpose of securing to her £4,500 of land in England and Gascony by way of dowry for her life.[1] In 1281 Christiana de Mariscis became a tenant[2] and very shortly afterwards Gregory de Rokesley, the Goldsmith, Mayor of London and Master of the Mint, was granted a lease for 10 years at a rent of £22 a year.[3] In 1284 Gilbert Peeche appears to have been given a life interest in the manor,[4] but the relations of these various interests are not clear. When Edward I married Margaret, the sister of the King of France, in 1299, the Manor of Banstead with the park was assigned to her and the grant was confirmed by his son Edward II.[5]

In 1318 the manor, which was valued at £30, was assigned as part of the dower of Queen Isabella in fulfilment of the arrangement made under the supervision of Pope Boniface VIII between Philip King of France, her father, and Edward I for her marriage to Edward II.[6]

In 1331 the Manor of Banstead with the park of the value of £30 was granted with other lands by Edward III to Queen Philippa as dower with the assent of Parliament and in fulfilment of the King's promise.[7] The manor house in 1336 was in a bad state of repair, and the two main walls of the hall threatened collapse, so that repairs were urgently required.[8]

In 1370 John Wortyng, who had been the King's bailiff at Banstead since 1354, took a lease of the manor,[9] but he died in or before 1376, and the Prior of Merton then farmed it.[10] The same year Nicholas de Carreu received a grant for life under Edward III, saving to the Prior the term granted to him. Carreu, who was Keeper of the Privy Seal, died in 1391.[11] Various

1 Calendar of Charter Rolls.
2 C. P. R. 22 Feb. 1281.
3 Abbrev. Rot. Orig. 10 Edw. I, Ro. 2.
4 Calendar Charter Rolls, 12 Feb. 1284.
5 See C. P. R. 19 March 1310.
6 C. P. R. 6 March 1318 and 1 Aug. 1318.
7 C. P. R. 1 Jan. 1331.
8 Inquisitions Miscellaneous, *c.* 145/130.
9 See i. 123, 90, and chapter II of this volume.
10 See i. 130, with account of repairs done.
11 See C. P. R. 6 March 1378 and M. B. ii. 583.

grants were made then and later from the issues of the manor to Royal servants, e.g. 43*s.* 4*d.* yearly to Laurence Daubernon, Groom of Queen Philippa's Chamber, and 100*s.* yearly to Stephen de Haddele, yeoman of her Chamber,[1] and 44*s.* a year to John Fraunceys, yeoman of the kitchen.[2]

In 1397 William de Arundell and Agnes his wife had a grant of the manor[3] in succession to Reginald Braibrok, knight, to whom the King had lately granted it for life,[4] and on William's death without issue his brother, the King's Knight, Richard Darrundell, had in 1401 a grant with lands in Wauton and Charlwode to the value of 80 marks yearly, provided he answered for any surplus. This grant was subsequently confirmed to Arundel and his wife Alice, who survived him.[5] Before his death in 1419 he had made himself very unpopular at Banstead, on account of what the poor tenants alleged to be his high-handed proceedings in enforcing his manorial rights.[6] His widow held the manor till her death in 1436, when the inquisition showed that there were £19 10*s.* of rents, 300 acres of arable worth 4*d.* an acre, a court baron and view of frankpledge worth 10*s.* a year, and a warren of rabbits worth 40*s.* yearly, besides a park which was worth nothing beyond the cost of fencing and feeding the deer.[7]

In 1437 the manors of Banstede and Wauton on the hill with certain lands in Charlwood were granted to Ralph Rochford, knight, for life with remainder to John Merston and Rose his wife, and in 1438 he received a license to lease them to the Merstons.[8]

In 1439 John Merston, the King's esquire (who held the Manor of Horton in Epsom) and Rose his wife received a licence to enclose the park, which was in great need of repair, with paling and hedge, and to cause trees and oaks to be felled yearly, without impeachment of waste, in the park and without it, in the lordship of Benstede, and in Wauton, under the

[1] C. P. R. 6 March and 10 May 1378.
[2] C. P. R. 6 July 1395.
[3] C. P. R. 31 Oct. 1399.
[4] C. P. R. 25 Oct. 1397.
[5] C. P. R. 27 Sep. 1401 and 18 Dec. 1423.
[6] See chapter IV.
[7] Exchequer, I. P. M., 15 Henry VI 161/15. The bank and ditch made for the medieval deer-fence can still be traced for a considerable distance round what is now Banstead Wood.
[8] C. P. R. 16 Nov. 1437 and 25 Jan. 1438.

survey of the Prior of Merton.[1] In 1449 the King's Sergeant, Richard Merston, Clerk of the Jewels, received a grant of the keeping of the Park of Benstede and warrens of Benestede and Waweton with the usual wages of *2d.* a day and *6d.* beyond from the issues of the lordship after the decease of John and Rose Merston.[2] The life interest of the Merstons was saved, when in 1449 an Act was passed[3] to confirm the grant by Letters Patent of these lands among others to the Provost and College Roial of our blessed Lady of Eton.[4] The manor, however, had no very lengthy connexion with Eton, for in 1464 Edward IV, who had little sympathy with his predecessors' foundation, procured an Act to resume the Manor of Banstead among a number of other manors. In 1465 he granted the Manors of Benestede and Walton to his Consort, Elizabeth, Queen of England, for her life in part support of her expenses in her chamber,[5] and in 1471 George Duke of Clarence received a life interest in the manor.[6] Henry VII settled it on his Queen Elizabeth.[7]

During the fifteenth century the manor, when not granted to private persons, appears to have always been farmed out. In 1482 the farmer was Nicholas Gaynsford,[8] Esquire of the body to Edward IV and Henry VII, who belonged to the family of Gaynsford of Crowhurst and lies buried in Carshalton Church.

The manors of Bansted and Walton with lands in Charlewode and Horley were granted to Queen Catherine as part of her dowry by Henry VIII in 1509. In February 1532 she leased them to Sir Nicholas Carew for 99 years and in June 1532 he received a grant in reversion at an annual rent of £40 to hold from the death of the Queen.[9]

The Queen died in 1536, but Carew, having been charged with

[1] C. P. R. 12 Nov. 1439. The Merston's tenure of Banstead Manor appears to have been interrupted by a Parliamentary Act of resumption and a fresh grant was made 12 March 1457 (C. P. R.).

[2] C. P. R. 10 July 1449.

[3] See Rolls of Parliament, v. 159.

[4] See Heywood and Wright, Ancient Laws for King's College, Cambridge and Eton, p. 465.

[5] See C. P. R. An Act of 7 & 8 Edw. IV (Rolls of Parlt. v. 624) validates the grant for life to Elizabeth.

[6] C. P. R. 23 March 1471.

[7] M. B. ii. 583.

[8] Ministers' Accounts, 1094/7.

[9] Letters and Papers, Henry VIII, vol. v, Grants, July 1532.

high treason, was in 1539 beheaded on Tower Hill. After his death an Act of Parliament was passed attainting him, together with the Marquis of Exeter and others, who had suffered execution. The manor, therefore, returned to the hands of the King, and by the Act 32 Henry VIII c. 55 was annexed with other manors to the Honour of Hampton Court.[1] Sir Ralph Sadler, afterwards Secretary of State, who was much employed in diplomatic work in Scotland, was appointed on 3 January 1541 to be steward of the manors of Nonesuche, Ewell, Eschaym, Weschaym, Sutton, Banstead, and Walton on the Hill,[2] and on 25 June 1541 he had a lease for 21 years of the manors of Banstead and Walton.[3] Sadler assigned to Sir Thomas Cawerden, and in March 1544 Sadler surrendered his patent of 3 January 1541, and Thomas Cawarden, a gentleman of the Privy Chamber, was appointed in his place.[4]

An Act of Parliament 'for the restitucion in bloude of Mr. Frauncis Carewe', the son of Sir Nicholas, was, however, passed after Henry's death (2 & 3 Edw. VI c. 3), and by Letters Patent of 14 January 1554 he received a grant of the manors of Bansted and Walton on the Hill in fee farm for ever for a rent of £40.[5]

Sir Francis Carew, who was famous for his magnificent gardens at Beddington[6] where he entertained Queen Elizabeth, lived till 1611, and left his Surrey estates, including the Manor of Banstead, to his nephew Nicholas Throckmorton, who took the name and arms of Carew, and died in 1644.[7] The manor descended in the Carew family till 1762, when Sir Nicholas Hackett Carew sold it for £15,000 to Mr. Rowland Frye of Wallington. Half of the fee farm rent of £40 was to be chargeable to the Manor of Banstead and the other half was to remain a charge on the Manor of Walton. Rowland Frye, who had spent the earlier part of his life in Virginia and Antigua, died in October 1777, and was succeeded by his brother William Frye, who died in 1795 and his nephew Rowland Frye who died in 1801. William Morris Newton, nephew of the last

[1] Letters and Papers, 1540. [2] See i. 166. [3] Letters and Papers.
[4] Letters and Papers, 1544. [5] Patent Roll 1 Mary.
[6] Some details of his house and garden expenses will be found in S. A. C. XXXI.
[7] M. B. ii. 527, who give a genealogical tree of Carew.

named, on succeeding took the name and arms of Frye, and died without issue in November 1820, after devising his estate for life to his sister, Mrs. Spencer, who in 1812 had married Mr. Henry Leigh Spencer. Her son Henry Newton Spencer died unmarried in 1836, and after her death her two surviving daughters sold the manor, in 1853, to Mr. Thomas Alcock of Kingswood. It was sold in 1873 to Sir John Hartopp and, after his bankruptcy, passed to his mortgagees, the Trustees of Lady Lavinia Bickersteth being the present lords. The park and demesne lands have been separated from the manor.

The Court Rolls begin in 1378 and continue with gaps to 1433, when they break off and only resume in 1486. The earlier rolls are dealt with in some detail in Chapters III and IV, and some specimen Courts have been printed in full in the Appendix, viz. Courts with View of 1378,[1] 1393, and 1412, and Courts of 1414 and 1433. The Tudor rolls form the subject of Chapter VI, and a Court of 1489,[1] one Court with View of Henry VIII (1533) and one of Elizabeth (1581) have also been printed in full.

It is now necessary to consider the smaller manors, Great Burgh, North Tadworth, South Tadworth, Perrotts, Little Borough, and Preston to which the fancy of draughtsmen sometimes, especially in Tudor times, made additions,

Great Burgh

The claim of Great Burgh (or Westburgh or Westborough) to be a real manor is unquestionable. Already in Domesday Book, Berge is held separately, Hugh de Port holding of the Bishop, and Great Burgh is undoubtedly one of the most ancient centres of settlement in Banstead.[2]

In the thirteenth century, according to the Testa de Nevill, John de Bures held one knight's fee in Berewe of the Honour of Munbray (either of the King or of Hubert de Burgh).[3] There

[1] These Courts are reprinted in vol. i.

[2] The name appears in a great variety of spelling, but it probably represents what is in modern English barrow (= Dutch and German berg) rather than what is in modern English borough (= Dutch and German burg) since the site which is at the top of a rise exactly fits and there is no trace of a fortified building.

[3] Testa de Nevill (1807), pp. 220, 221.

can be no doubt that Great Burgh was then regarded as being a subinfeudation of Banstead, for in the Inquisition held on the death of John de Bures in 1276[1] it is said that he held in chief of the King by knight service by reason of the Manor of Banstead, which then belonged to the King. And in the Extent of 1325 John de Burs appears among the free tenants as holding Berghe for one Knight's fee and owing *2s.* rent and suit of Court,[2] and similarly Robert Moyce (Moys) in the rental of 1598. In 1384 the manor passed into the hands of Thomas Hayton,[3] and in 1466 to Henry Merland, whose descendants conveyed in 1615 to Christopher Buckle, whose family held till the middle of last century. It was purchased in 1846 by Lord Egmont, and subsequently by Mr. F. E. Colman,[4] becoming merged in what is now known as the Nork Estate.

No Court Rolls appear to have survived.

North Tadworth

North Tadworth, which is probably identical with the Tadorne of Domesday, though not shown in 1086 as a subinfeudation of Banstead, probably was so.[5] In the Testa de Nevill William Hansard held two knights' fees in Tadworth from Hubert de Burgh of the Honour of Mowbray, and these were no doubt North and South Tadworth. The former was given by his sons to the Priory of St. Mary Overey at Southwark[6] and was held by the Convent together with the rectory till the Dissolution.

The history of the Convent's tenure is almost a blank. But the Priory appears to have been accustomed for long before the Dissolution to let their lands,[7] and when the Dissolution occurred Richard Moys held a lease for forty years from 1524 of the Manor of North Tadworth and the Rectory with the mansion of the same at Southmerfeld.[8] His account for 1539–40 is indeed headed 'Manors of Northtadworth and Southmerfeld' but there is no reason to suppose that the latter was a

[1] Chancery, I. P. M., 4 Edw. I, 19.

[2] i. 64, 183. See also 157. But the survey of Banstead Manor in 1680 (see i. 198) treats Great Burgh as outside Banstead.

[3] See i. 153. [4] See details in V. H. S. iii. 256. [5] See i. 28.

[6] V. H. S. iii. 258. [7] i. 163. [8] i. 174.

separate manor, and in a petition to the Chancellor of about this date he describes himself, no doubt correctly, as 'fermor . . . of the parsonage of Bansted with the mancyon of Summerfeld and the manor of North Tadworthe'.[1]

The manor was acquired from the heirs of Richard Moys by Christopher Buckle in 1663,[2] and was subsequently held with Great Burgh[3] and sold with it in 1846 to Lord Egmont.

No Court Rolls are known to exist.

South Tadworth

South Tadworth must be the Tadeorde of Domesday, and the other Tadworth held for a knight's fee by William Hansard in the Testa de Nevill. Like North Tadworth it passed into the hands of a religious house, the Priory of Merton, at some date before 1274,[4] and it remained in the possession of the Convent till the Dissolution. It was then held by John Steward on a lease of 21 years from 1535.[5] After being temporarily annexed to the Honour of Hampton Court it was acquired by Edward Herrenden in 1553 whose heirs sold it in 1620, since which date it has never been held in any family for any considerable time.[6] The most remarkable owners were Leonard Wessel, who about 1700 built the fine house known as Tadworth Court, and whose daughter Sarah married Christopher Buckle, who built Nork House, and Lord Russell of Killowen. After Lord Russell's death in 1900, the house was sold but not the manor. The house was bought in 1926 by the Hospital for Sick Children (Great Ormond Street) for the purpose of a branch hospital.

The Court Rolls go back to 1394 though not continuously, and some account of the earlier rolls will be found in Chapter V.

[1] Proceedings of the Court of Augmentations, 33/15.

[2] See V. H. S. iii. 258.

[3] Thus the marriage settlement (22 May 1766) of Christopher Buckle of Burrough in Banstead and Mary Neave, refers to the 'manors or reputed manors of Borrow alias West burgh alias Westborrow, Preston, Little Borrow and North Tadworth' and to 'all that the Rectory of Bansted called Cannons alias Southmerfield alias Summerfield'.

[4] V. H. S. iii. 258.

[5] i. 171.

[6] For the various holders see V. H. S. iii. 258.

Chaldon

Chaldon is mentioned in Domesday with Banstead, and in the Extent of 1325 the first tenant is Sir John Covert, who holds at Chalvedone one knight's fee and he owes for rent 6*s.* and will do suit of Court from three weeks to three weeks. In the rental of 1598 the first tenant is John Southcut, who holds the Manor of Chaldon for one knight's fee and 6*s.* rent.[1] Between these dates the Court Roll shows a tithing man for Chaldon at view of frankpledge, and many cases of fines imposed on the tenants of the manor for default of suit.[2] At a Court of 1 October 1638 the death of John Southcott, who held freely by knight service for one knight's fee the Manor of Chaldon, paying 6*s.* annually, was presented, the heriot being an ox worth £5 and the relief £5. In 1580, however, the manor, when purchased by John Southcott, Justice of the Queen's Bench, was described as held of the honour of Rochester Castle.[3] There was an old connexion with Rochester, and Chaldon paid Castle guard like South Tadworth (see p. 49) to Rochester Castle. But whatever the explanation of this, it seems clear that Chaldon was held of Banstead.

Perrotts

Great Burgh, North and South Tadworth, and Chaldon are all mentioned in Domesday. The unnamed subinfeudations cannot be identified. The earliest reference to the Manor of Perrotts by name is in 1447 when the Court Roll begins. The manor was held in 1461 by William Charlwood. In 1489 the Banstead Court Roll shows that John Charlwood enfeoffed Richard Colcok and others, evidently trustees, of his lands called Parotts in Bansted, and Colcok did fealty for them, and in 1507 Alexander Charlwood paid a relief of 3*s.* to Banstead for a parcel of land called Perrotts, rent 2*s.* a year, formerly

[1] See i. 30, 63, and 183.

[2] The Court of 10 Dec. 1504 contains a good instance, as the homage presented that the tenants of the manors of Chaldon, Westburgh, and of the land of Perrottis, with Robert Shirborn and various other individuals were Suitors of the Court, and made default of suit of Court. They were all fined.

[3] See V. H. S. iv. 189. The account of Chaldon there ignores the connexion with Banstead. But see also M. B. ii. 441.

belonging to his father Thomas. In 1516 Alexander Charlwood sold the manor to John Lambert,[1] whose descendants held it till 1921, when it was sold to Mr. C. H. Garton.

Some remarks on the Court Roll will be found in Chapter V, and some of the earlier Courts are printed in the Appendix. The manor was very small, covering Perrott's farm and Read's Rest.

Little Burgh

The Manor of Little Burgh appears in the survey of 1598 as held by Humphrey Covert and paying a rent of 23*s.* 6*d.* to Banstead. But in 1541 it was not called a manor, but was described more fully as two virgates of land containing 200 acres called Lytle Barrow lying in the parish of Banstead and held by Richard Covert.[2] It is evidently identical with the two virgates held freely by Henry de Bergh in 1325 which paid 23*s.* 6*d.* and 1 lb. of cummin (also referred to in 1541).[3] In deeds relating to the Buckle property (Great Burgh, &c.), in which it was merged, it is included among the other 'manors or reputed manors' held by that family (see e.g. the quotation of 1766 under North Tadworth). But no Court Rolls exist, or as far as is known, ever have existed, and its status as a manor seems doubtful, even if we remember that in the Middle Ages it was not clear how far a manor connoted jurisdiction.[4] At the survey of 1680 eighty acres of the lands of Little Burgh are entered,[5] though none of the lands of the undoubted manors (Great Burgh, &c.) are recorded. But this is inconclusive, and may only mean that the owner, who claimed it as a manor, kept most of the land off the record.

Preston

Preston appears in the fourteenth century as held by the Chetwode family, and from them passed to the Merlands, by whom and their successors, the Buckles, it was held with Great Burgh. But the parish of Preston was once a Peculiar of the

[1] The history of the transaction, which began in 1513 and was not finally completed till 1520, with a description of the documents, is given in S. A. C. xxxii.

[2] i. 168.

[3] i. 64.

[4] See Holdsworth, History of English Law, i. 180, 181.

[5] i. 199, 284.

See of Canterbury,[1] as is clearly established by the evidence of the Lambeth registers, which speak of the parish church of Preston as of the Deanery of Croydon and as 'immediate jurisdictionis domini' (1317), and when Richard Merland died, who held the Manor of Preston with the advowson of the Church of St. Leonard belonging to that manor, it was stated in the Inquisition p.m. in 1506 that the manor was held of the Archbishop of Canterbury as of his lordship or Manor of Croydon.

This is borne out by the Curia Regis roll of 1206, where a case is recorded between Osbert the Chaplain and Stephen Norwode and Fediva his wife concerning three virgates in Preston and a hide in Berges, in the course of which it appears that the steward of the Archbishop of Canterbury had claimed and exercised jurisdiction.[2] But no evidence is available to show either when the archbishop acquired the manor or when he parted with it, or even to show when the parish ceased to be a Peculiar, the latest entry in the Lambeth registers being of 1482. All recollection of the connexion with Canterbury seems to have faded away.

It is, according to Wood who wrote the Institute of the Laws of England, a standard work till superseded by Blackstone, an ancient privilege of the See of Canterbury that whenever any manors or advowsons belong to it they forthwith become exempt from the Ordinary, and are reputed Peculiars of that See.[3] The Archbishop seems, in fact, to have held lands before the Conquest in all the eleven other Surrey parishes which before the nineteenth century were separated from the See of Winchester,[4] so though the Archbishop in the fourteenth century held neither manor nor advowson, it would seem probable that, as in the case of the other Peculiars, he had held the manor before the Conquest.

No Court Rolls are known to have survived, nor any record

[1] See S. A. C. xxxvii. 71, quoting the evidence from the Registers collected by Mr. G. W. Waine. The earliest presentation is of 1317 and the latest 1482.

[2] See Curia Regis Rolls, iv. 264, with earlier references. In the Rotuli Curie Regis (1835), i. 356, there is a case of 1199 relating to a hide and three virgates in Preston, in which proceedings in the Archbishop's Court appear. That entry is headed Kent (as is one of those in the later proceedings), but Kent appears to be an error.

[3] Cited by J. under Peculiar.

[4] See V. H. S. ii. 3.

of the exact extent of the manor. But if we add to Preston Preston Hatch, Preston Haw, Preston Banks, Preston Orchard, and Preston Meadow, which all appear on the tithe map, Chapel Grove, where are the foundations of St. Leonard's, and the Knolls, Grubbed piece, Rose bushes, Parson's bush piece and Nork, all of which are stated in the seventeenth century map in my possession (see p. 78) to be parcel of the lordship of Preston, it seems that it stretched from the South Tadworth boundary, represented on the tithe map by the boundary of Tadworth Tithing, nearly to Warren Farm (which was itself in the Manor of Great Burgh), Preston Downs marching with Ewell Downs on the West. But whatever its earlier importance it was its fate to be dwarfed by Great Burgh with which it was held.

II

THE MANOR IN 1353–4

JOHN WORTYNG was bailiff of the manor for many years, finally taking a lease in 1369 for ten years. When the first volume of this book was published no earlier account than that of 1363–4 was known to exist, but an account for 1353–4 has now been discovered at the Record Office.[1] It had been used as a wrapper for another document, and has in places been damaged by damp, but most of it is in fair condition, and the general form and substance are clear. It is not only interesting in itself, but it helps to bridge the gap between the elaborate Extent of 1325 and Wortyng's accounts beginning in 1363.

The form of the account is, except in a few details, the same as in the later accounts. Under receipts the Rents of Assize and Sale of Labour are identical with those of 1363–4, nor do the minor headings (dairy, pleas of Court, &c.) differ much. On the expenditure side the ordinary maintenance charges, wages and cost of harvest are much the same as in 1363–4, the largest difference being that only 2*s.* 2*d.* were spent on repairs to buildings against £6 17*s.* 3½*d.* in 1363–4. But the total of receipts is only £39 4*s.* 9⅜*d.* against £105 10*s.* 3⅛*d.*, the reason for which may have been a bad season the year before. The sale of corn was only £4 1*s.* 7¾*d.* against £44 14*s.* 1*d.* in 1363–4, and sale of stock including woolfells only £2 3*s.* 8*d.* against £6 17*s.* 8½*d.* for stock and £11 14*s.* 1*d.* for wool. It is, however, clear that we have not the whole story on the account, for though the account runs from the day after Michaelmas 1353 it appears that the corn (20 quarters of wheat and 67 quarters of oats with taricorn, barley, peas, vetches and dredge) and live stock were only delivered to Wortyng on 31 December 1353 by John Coke, Treasurer of Philippa, Queen of England (who then held the manor) by indenture. This is no doubt the reason why it is expressly stated that there is nothing for thrashing in this account. The account of the live stock looks

[1] Spec. Coll. Ministers' Accounts, 1010/11.

less unfavourable, for Wortyng began with 587 sheep and lambs and ended with 544, shearing 477 fleeces against 552 in 1363–4. But he was not able to sell his wool, for he was left with his 477 fleeces weighing two sacks.[1] The other animals show very similar numbers in the two accounts.[2]

The most interesting part of the account is, however, that which relates to tenements vacant owing probably to the Black Death, and relet on new conditions. Wortyng claimed £6 9*s*. 10*d*.[3] for allowance for vacant tenements, entering among his receipts 9*s*. 9½*d*. for those that were relet. These entries are struck out and a marginal note added 'Cancelled until inquiry is made how many and what tenements are in the Queen's hands, and for how much he could have answered on the issues of each tenement'. Nicholas de Careu, acting for the Steward, Fyfhide, was to inquire and certify. Attached to the foot of the third membrane, which is blank, is the record of an Inquisition held at the manor Court on 28 October 1354, which is reprinted in full in the Appendix with a few words (shown in brackets) supplied from the Account. This Inquisition shows a failure of rent in the case of 27 holdings, all of which appear to have been held by separate tenants. Some, e.g. Soleland[4] may have been lying vacant because of the poverty of the soil, but the list gives no indication of the causes, and in some cases where the tenant had died of the Black Death he had no doubt been succeeded by his heir. In any case 27 is an upper limit for the number of holdings remaining vacant owing to the death of tenants. The Extent of 1325 shows 78 villein holdings in Banstead and 27 in the Weald, or 105 in all (of which 2 at Banstead and 1 in the Weald were then vacant), so if we may assume that the number of holdings remained approximately the same, which is probable as many of the 1325 names are used, we get, say, a quarter of the holdings as the largest possible number of holdings vacant in 1353 owing to the Black Death. But such a figure is only reached by ascribing everything to the

[1] See i. 95.

[2] The stotti of the later accounts appear as affri, i.e. horses which were not cart-horses.

[3] This is the figure in the margin of the document, but the addition is, as so often, not quite correct.

[4] It was vacant in the Extent of 1325 and unlet in 1365 (i. 86, 97).

plague, and though any figure can only be a guess this seems too great.[1]

The number of customary tenants for whom food had to be provided at two Waterbedrepes in 1353–4 was 131 (in 1363–4 it was 144), but this figure is not comparable with that of the holdings, as it includes men such as the eight whom John le Longe had to bring with him (i. 76).

The land thrown on the lady's hands was, of course, as far as possible relet, and it will be seen that this was done in every case for a term of years, six years apparently when the lease was granted by the Steward, or one if granted by the Bailiff. In no case is any mention made of rents and services other than the fixed money rent. Godesone for instance, who took John Longe's virgate, not only paid less rent than Long was assessed at, but was presumably free of all his complicated obligations (see i. 76). If it was difficult to enforce the old obligations in a case like this, it must have been quite impossible when a tenement was broken up, as often happened, e.g. three separate tenants took parts of William atte Strete's tenement, and two took parts of each of three different Cole tenements—possibly a case of a family being wiped out by the Black Death.

The tenements referred to are some of them in Banstead, and some in the Weald (e.g. Alice Boyton's land), but mostly at Banstead, which had a much larger population than the part of the manor in the Weald.

[1] At Godstone all the suitors at the mill were said to have died in 1349 (Lambert, Godstone, p. 112). In the Hundred of Farnham, from a third to a half of the population is supposed to have died (English Historical Review, Oct. 1929, p. 571). The figures, no doubt, varied greatly from place to place.

III

THE BANSTEAD COURT ROLL IN THE REIGNS OF RICHARD II AND HENRY IV

THE roll begins in May 1378, and breaks off in 1380, but parts of 1383 and 1384, and of 1393 and 1394 are preserved, making eighteen Courts in the reign of Richard II. In the reign of Henry IV the roll begins in 1401 and is fairly continuous to 1409, after which there is a gap until 1411. It then runs to the end of the reign, making thirty Courts in this reign, or forty-eight in all.[1]

The manor, which at this time belonged to the King, having been obtained by Edward I as part of an exchange of lands with Sir John de Burgh, son of the great Justiciar, embraced, as we have seen, besides Banstead itself a considerable part of the parishes of Horley and Leigh. These parts in the Weald sent a separate homage to the Banstead Manor Court. Chaldon and some land in Wallington, which were also held of Banstead, had separate tithing-men.

The Manor Court, which possessed both criminal and civil jurisdiction of a limited kind, and, as we shall see, was valuable to the lord both as a source of revenue and for protecting his interests, is described on the roll simply as 'Curia', with 'Banstede' in the margin, except when the View of Frank-pledge was held once a year (usually in the autumn), when the description 'Curia cum visu' is used. The only case of a more elaborate heading is a Court in December 1401, which is headed 'Visus franci plegii cum prima curia domini Ricardi de Arundell Chivaler'. The King's knight, Richard Darrundell, brother of William Darrundell, chivaler, who was just dead, had received on 27 September 1401 a grant from the King of the manor, with the knight's fees, park, and warren for life, to the value

[1] The Court with View of 4 November 1378 is printed in full in i. 537, with translation, p. 139. (Note 2 on p. 156 is not correct.) The Courts with View of 27 Oct. 1393 and of 27 Sept. 1412 are printed in the Appendix to this volume. As a rule the View precedes the Court, which begins with 'modo de curia', but not always. On 27 Sept. 1412, a curia cum visu begins with the ordinary Court, and then Visus follows.

of 80 marks yearly, provided that he answered for any surplus. William had similarly held Banstead, and before him another King's knight, Reginald Braibrok, had held it, and at the beginning of the reign of Richard II it was held for life by Nicholas de Carreu, so that it would seem that at no time during the years covered by the rolls was the manor in the King's own hands.

The names of both William and Richard Arundel appear frequently on the Patent Rolls of the time as engaged on the King's service; e.g. in March 1405 Richard had to garrison Hay with sixteen men-at-arms and eighty archers when the King was going to chastise the rebels in Wales.

The View of Frankpledge is also called on the rolls a leet, e.g. at the View of 1404 the tithing-man for Chaldon is fined 6*d*. because he did not come to present the 'articulos letis'. It was in theory a Court of criminal jurisdiction,[1] and as such is always distinguished on the rolls from the ordinary court. The main distinction in practice is that the various tithing-men appear for their tithings and pay the common fine or borghsilver[2] at the rate of 1*d*. a head for the other members[3] of their tithings, each of whom was supposed to be security for the others, and directions are given for enrolling defaulters in their proper tithings. No transfers of land or ordinary litigation were conducted at the View, but the presentations made by the tithing-men, e.g. for breach of the assize of ale (which at Banstead itself were made by a special officer, the Aletaster, and in the outlying parts by the tithing-men) or for nuisances such as the flooding of roads owing to the failure of a tenant to clean his ditches, differ little from similar presentations made at the ordinary Courts.

The manor was divided into fourteen or fifteen tithings. Banstead itself had five (in 1378 it had six) tithings, and Tad-

[1] See Holdsworth, History of English Law, i. 135.

[2] From the Anglo-Saxon 'Bohr', or security. See Holdsworth, i. 14.

[3] The tithing-man seems to have been exempt, for in 1406 the tithing-man of Leangre simply presents that all is well and pays nothing. In the Tooting Beck Court Rolls (published by the London County Council, 1909) at this time when the tithing-man pays his borghsilver 'capitaneo deducto' is added, but this is not so stated in the Banstead roll. The tithing-man for Wallington at the Banstead Court of 21 Oct. 1533 (p. 99) paid 1*d*. for himself.

worth and Copthill, both of which are in the present civil parish, each had one. So had Chaldon and Wallington, and the parts of the manor below the hill (the Weald), viz. Sidlow Mill, Horley, Leigh, Hyde, and Hulle (the latter after 1400 is called Leangre). The amount of borgh-silver paid in 1378 was 7*s.* 10*d.* (the Chaldon entry is, however, illegible). If we add 3*d.* for Chaldon (which is what it paid in 1393) and 1*s.* 3*d.* for the fifteen tithing-men, we get 9*s.* 4*d.*, which at 1*d.* a head gives 112 members of the tithings. There were also four defaults. The total is larger than in subsequent Views, where the figures tend to drop.

The Court was presided over by the steward, who represented the lord. He is not mentioned in these rolls, except that there is an entry in 1411 of the cost of his dinner, viz. 2*d.* in bread, 1½*d.* in beer, and 3*d.* in meat. But the formula used for judgements, 'ideo consideratum est quod . . .' (it was adjudged that . . .) or 'consideratum est per curiam', represents the steward's pronouncement, and in the contemporary Tooting Court Rolls the formula used is 'ideo consideratum est per senescallum'.[1]

The officer of the Court, whose business it was to see to summonses, distraints, &c., was the bedel, and service in the appointment, which was obligatory on villeins, was not popular. In 1404 the tenants in the Weald claimed to be exempt from serving as bedel, and in the reign of Henry V all the tenants claimed to be exempt. The bedel was liable to fine for failure to distrain properly when ordered by the Court; e.g. in 1408 he is fined 2*d.* for failing to distrain the Prior of St. Mary Overey, who was required to prove his title to Collinsland in Banstead. The work was at best troublesome, and perhaps sometimes dangerous. In 1407 the wife of a poaching tenant is fined 4*d.* for making a rescue from the bedel, and it must in any case have interfered seriously with the bedel's own business. He had, however, allowances,[2] besides which he received occasional pickings. In 1393 orders were given to distrain in a case of debt, and the bedel seized a dish and pot worth 3*s.*, of which for his zeal he was granted 3*d.* But this seems to have been exceptional. The bedel was known later in Banstead as Constable,

[1] e.g. p. 134, Tooting Beck Court Rolls.
[2] See Wortyng's account, i. 122.

and the tithing-men as Headboroughs (but in Tadworth as Constable). A bailiff is also referred to as arresting strays, but he does not otherwise appear. The bailiff was originally responsible for farming operations,[1] and the bedel had also been an agricultural servant.[2] It is possible that the offices were now combined. In any case, both officials appear to have become merely officers of the Court.

The Court also appointed Affeerers, who reduced to a precise sum the fines resulting from decisions of the Court. Affeerers vary from court to court, being evidently appointed for the particular sitting, and are generally two, but sometimes three, and occasionally four, in number.

One other manorial officer is referred to on the roll, viz. the reeve (prepositus), an officer who in 1277 had rendered account of all receipts and expenditure in the manor,[3] but is now (1408) only called a collector of rent. He does not play any part on the roll.

Let us now consider what purposes the Court actually served. In the first place, it enabled the lord to collect his dues, and served to protect his interests. At every View the borghsilver is paid; miscellaneous payments, such as evese[4] (payment of ½*d.* for each pig) or deodands, are collected at the ordinary Court, and there is hardly a court at which some of the tenants were not fined the customary 2*d.* for breaking the assize of beer —a payment so regular that it seems to be rather a licence than a penalty. The bondman who resided outside the manor paid

[1] i. 90.

[2] i. 41. The Carshalton Court Rolls printed by the Surrey Record Society show the bailiff making distraints, &c., which are made at Banstead by the bedel in these two reigns.

[3] i. 45.

[4] Or avisagium. Evese is wrongly printed in the Extent of 1325 (i. 321 and 69) as enese. Also grasanes paid by tenants in the Weald (p. 320). See also p. 349, where it is given as garsanes (1364). n and v are indistinguishable in the handwriting of the Extent, but the use of avisagium or avesagium in the Court Roll and the verb avesare, and indeed the form aves' porcorum (e.g. in 1408) show that the correct words are evese and grasaves. Aves Courts and aves rents or pannage rents are found in Sussex, the customary tenants in Ashdown Forest paying Gersheues (V. H. Sussex ii. 314, 320, 321). In Kent at Boughton Aluph eueshale, or auesinghale, existed (Neilson, Cartulary and Survey of Bilsington, pp. 16 and 37), and Blount (quoted by J.) says that avage or avisage was a payment by tenants of the Manor of Writtle in Essex for pannage in the lord's woods for pigs.

his chevage, the tenant who did not wish to attend Court paid for being let off, heriots are collected on death and fines on admission to tenements. In addition to payments like these of the nature of dues, there were fines in our sense for defaulting in attendance at Court or failing to carry out the directions of the Court. The Court was, in fact, a profitable possession and more than paid its expenses. The tenants attended compulsorily and without payment, offenders who were guilty, e.g. of assault, were fined, not imprisoned, and unsuccessful litigants always paid a fine to the Court.[1] The Courts with View produced, of course, most money—that of 1404 produced £2 1*s.* 3*d.*, of which borghsilver was 5*s.* 9*d.*

But the Court was also useful to the lord in protecting his interests in many ways. Thus it is presented in 1406 that Cecily Hened has occupied a piece of land without the lord's leave and for the past thirty years has withdrawn the rent—this she disputed—and that John Hereward has withdrawn his harvest labour for four years—he was fined 6*d.* at the next Court.

There are continual presentments about poaching, e.g. in 1403 that Roger Cokeman of Blecchyngelegh and Richard Tyler of the same came into the lord's park and warren with bows and arrows, dogs and other devices, to hunt his deer and rabbits. In 1404 John Dyg, clerk, apparently an ex-vicar of Banstead, was fined no less than 6*s.* 8*d.* for trespassing in the lord's warren. In the same year seven tenants are fined in a batch for trespassing with their cattle, pigs, or horses on the lord's pasture, and Thomas atte Mere, who has cut down oaks and other trees in le Swynefeldysgrene to the grave loss of the lord, must answer for it. The Court supplied the machinery through which tenants were compelled to keep the lord's buildings and their own tenements in repair. The homage of Banstead

[1] At a Court in 1383 are two cases of pleas of debt in each of which the defendant admitted the debt and an order was made that the plaintiff should recover the debt and damages claimed. The bedel was to distrain the defendant to satisfy the plaintiff, and 'respondere domino de quolibet xijd. id. secundum consuetudinem manerii', i.e. the lord was entitled to take 1*d.* in the shilling for enforcing the judgement. In addition, one of the defendants, like other unsuccessful litigants, was fined 2*d.* for losing his case.

and of the Weald have a day to repair the lord's grange (1402), and it is presented that John Woghere unroofed a barn on his bond tenement which was roofed with Horsham slates, and carried the aforesaid stones to the demesne of the Prior of Merton, and he is to be distrained to answer the lord for the waste (1401). In 1378 there is an entry fixing the date by which John Hend had to do his repairs, with a note that he had in his possession and was answerable to the lord for two stones, one oak, two boards, one frame, three racks for sheep, a bushel and a seed-basket—apparently a case where the lord had made an advance. This, however, is unusual, it usually being presented merely that a tenement is ruinous and that the tenant must repair it.

All this was legitimate, but the lord, who in 1393 makes a claim on the roll to appoint the bedel, either as against a claim that the appointment was elective or because he knew of the objection of some of the tenants to serve, at times strained the machinery of the Court. There seems to be a clear case of this in 1406, when it is recorded that orders were given to all tenants of Banstede who held according to the custom of the manor that in future their dogs should be expeditated under a penalty of 100*s*. Now the expeditation of dogs, or cutting out the ball of the forefeet for the preservation of the King's game, is a term used in the laws of the forest, and there cannot have been any justification for such an order at Banstead in 1406. Before Richard Arundell's time there are entries indicating that the homage are responsible for fugitive bondmen, and this was no doubt common form.[1] But Arundell evidently tightened the machinery. In 1402 thirty-two names appear in one entry as doing fealty, which they would hardly have done in this way without some special cause.

In 1408 there are some remarkable entries on the roll. The Banstead homage then presented that Joan atte Mere, daughter of John atte Mere, had married John Tabard, and Emma another daughter, had married John Tayllour, without the lord's leave; and at the next Court Juliana atte Mere, daughter of William atte Mere, asks leave to marry Roger Thurston and pays £5 for permission (merchet), and at the same time the roll

[1] Cf. the case of Carter (1402) in the Tooting Roll.

records an acknowledgement of villenage by William Kyng with a description of his children. In 1412, after a similar record about the Bode family, Robert atte Mere, the lord's bondman, and all the bond homage are fined 10*s*. for failing to produce William Bode and other fugitive bondmen and threatened with a further penalty of 20*s*. if they fail again. We know that the tenants disputed the lord's view of their status, for the roll shows that in 1404 four of them refused to do fealty to the lord because they said that they were of free, not bond, status ('libere condicionis non native'), and all the tenants subsequently petitioned Henry V against Arundell's proceedings.[1] Whatever the legal rights of the parties to the dispute may have been, it is impossible to believe that the homage would have made such presentments as those of 1408 except under strong pressure.

The Court, however, served a number of useful purposes, both for the manor as a whole and for the individual tenant. Nuisances are constantly presented—the highway between Horsehulle and Leggersland is under water and foundrous by Richard Logger's default; John Huwet has not cleaned his ditches at Caldecroft (in Horley) and the road there is consequently foundrous (the roads in the Weald were always bad); the bridge below the church at Leigh is ruinous and should be repaired; Thomas Yhurst has ploughed up the road to Burgh; John Saunder has closed a lawful path (legalem semitam) at Tadworth; the highway at Sherwode Strete is foundrous owing to the digging of Thomas at Wode,[2] and so forth.

Also waifs and strays are dealt with, the latter being usually animals which gave little trouble. In 1378 it is solemnly recorded that a pair of boots came as waif (i.e. abandoned by a felon). In 1404 a black horse caused trouble. The horse was presented by one of the Banstead tithing-men as waif, but subsequently twelve tenants on their oath declared that the horse 'non fuit weyfyatum', or in the hands of a felon, and the

[1] See p. 32. The Extent of 1325 gives the name of one tenant in the Weald (i. 67) of whom the obligation not to marry a daughter without licence is specially recorded, which certainly seems to imply that the case was exceptional.

[2] Not long before iron had been mined in the highway at Horley. See S. A. C. xxxiv. 105.

tithing-man and his tithing were fined 6*d*. for a false presentation. In 1402 a sow gave rise to a conflict of jurisdictions. The Court testified that John Heed, late the lord's bailiff, arrested a sow of red and white colour within the lordship as stray in the 21st year of Richard II, but Stephen Ingram, the bailiff of the Hundred of Copthorne, took and removed the sow, to the lord's damage, &c., and let there be a writ, &c. But the result does not appear. In 1405 a black ox, aged two years, worth more than 10*s*., came as a stray and was seized by John the bailiff of the Hundred of Reygate 'vi et armis'.[1] And the same John broke the fence of John Tanner at Horley and took away two cows worth 20*s*. But though 10*s*. is written over the bailiff's name as if that was the fine which he was to pay, it is unlikely that he paid much attention to the Manor Court.

The Court interfered vigorously at times to protect the public. In 1406 one of the Banstead tithing-men presented that John Doveton, clerk, keeps a dog which bites various animals, and the comparatively heavy fine of half a mark (3*s*. 4*d*.) is imposed. The public opinion of a community of farmers regarding a dog which worried sheep was probably expressed by the Court. In 1412 the tithing-man of Sidlow mill presents that John Grenyng (who had been within the lordship for over a year without being placed in his tithing) was a common butcher taking excessive gain, and Grenyng is fined 2*d*., no doubt as a warning. The numerous presentments with regard to obstruction of roads have already been referred to.

But probably the greatest advantage which the Court gave to the tenant was that it supplied him with a convenient system of conveyance and land registration. Most of the business of the ordinary courts (as opposed to the View), which is not concerned with litigation is concerned with the conveyance of land held in villenage, or, as it was now in process of becoming, copyhold land. The free tenant was independent of

[1] We need not, of course, suppose that the words were literally true. As early as 1310 they were coming to be regarded as common form (Holdsworth, ii. 364). At one time they were, it would seem, employed to found jurisdiction in the King's Court by making what was a mere tort appear to be a breach of the King's peace. They became so firmly established that an Act of Parliament was passed in 1705 to make it safe to omit them in certain cases.

his lord's Court and could resort to the Royal Courts to protect his interests,[1] but the title to land held in villenage was to be found on the Court Roll, and such land had to be conveyed subject to the custom of the manor. When Cecily Hened's title to a virgate of land called Crouchelond was challenged, she produced in Court in 1407 a copy of an entry by which John Hened surrendered the virgate, and the lord re-granted it to John and Cecily and their heirs to be held by the ancient rents and services. The system of taking such copies was evidently thoroughly established. When, for instance, Robert Ihurst surrendered a messuage and half a virgate called Bechelond and Thomas Popelot was admitted in 1402, there is a note in the margin 'fiat copia', and the roll has the word 'copia' in the margin against a transfer of land in 1378. On every conveyance or admission to a tenement held in villenage the lord took his fees. There seems to have been a scale for admission of 3*s.* 4*d.*, or 6*s.* 8*d.*, or 13*s.* 4*d.*, but it is difficult to see on what principle the scale was applied, unless on that of the ability of the tenant to pay, and especially later the fines vary greatly. When, for instance, in 1393 John Lamput takes a virgate formerly belonging to John Long (a bondman who had left the manor without leave) for ten years for the ancient rents, services, and customs, and undertakes to do the repairs, he only pays a fine of 7*d.* for entry, and it seems clear that the lord was glad to admit for a purely nominal fine. On the other hand, in 1383, when Peter in the lane, who held a half-virgate and a farthing-land, died, the lord not only took as heriot an ox worth 13*s.* 4*d.*, but made his son John pay a fine of 6*s.* 8*d.* for admission. And he took his fees for every transaction. Thus, in 1412, when Margaret atte Mere died, who held for life a half-virgate formerly belonging to Thomas atte Mere, with reversion to Thomas's son Peter, the lord took a sheep worth 14*d.* as heriot and admitted Peter for a fine of 3*s.* 4*d.*; and when Peter thereupon surrendered the land and it was regranted to him and his wife, a further fine of 2*s.* was taken. These fines, however, although it is difficult to say on what exact principle they were levied, do not seem to be oppressive, being similar to the fines recorded at the time on the Tooting Roll.

[1] See Holdsworth, ii. 260.

We have seen that Arundell insisted on the conditions of villenage, and most of the admissions and conveyances are for the ancient rents, services, and customs. But he could not always let in this way. For instance, in 1406 Thomas Popelot took from the lord a tenement called Stretislond which was a half-virgate of twelve acres, also a garden of a quarter of an acre, and another half-acre, paying a rent of 5*s*. for all services and a fine of only 12*d*. for admission.

Although, however, the Court Roll afforded a decisive and convenient record of title, it was in one way unsatisfactory. No plans or maps, of course, existed, and in most cases no attempt was made to define boundaries. If any attempt is made to define position it is extremely rough. When Margery Popellot in 1378 surrenders three and a half acres not lying together, they are perforce described for identification, but only in the vaguest way, one at Leggeswaye and two and a half by the high road and called Marchalesland. In 1404 a single acre is let, and it is described as lying in Holdene (Holding Shot, no doubt, in Banstead Commonfield) between the land of the tenement le Frenoke on the south and the land of the tenement le Grete on the north. And this is unusually detailed. It was no doubt only because everybody knew every acre in the parish that disputes did not more often arise. But they did arise, and presently we shall come across an indirect method of deciding a title to land.

The Court Roll no doubt prevented much litigation as to title, but there are a few pleas of land recorded, mostly abandoned, with the result that the plaintiff was fined 2*d*.—perhaps a fairly inexpensive way of being disagreeable for a time to an unpleasant neighbour. There is, however, in 1404 a record of an elaborate plea of land in which Roger atte Hulle recovers land from William Kyng. They put themselves on the homage, who give an elaborate history of the land, showing that Kyng had lawfully held the land which he acquired from William atte Hulle and conveyed to John atte Hulle, who conveyed to Roger, the plaintiff, whom Kyng disseised unjustly and without judgement after King Henry's first voyage to Gascony[1] to the damage of Roger atte Hulle of 20*s*. So atte

[1] This is a reference to the statute of Edward I dealing with writs of novel disseisin. See the Recoveries printed in S. A. C. xxxii.

Hulle has entry on paying a fine of 6*s*. 8*d*. and gets the damages, and Kyng is fined 6*d*. The case may be real litigation, but it looks like a fictitious suit. In 1404 there is a quarrel about a right of way which Isabella atte Mere claimed against Henry Blake. In this case the Court, with the consent of the parties, made a compromise, giving the old lady the easement for her life on condition that she paid Blake a rent of a chicken every year.

The Manor Court probably modelled itself as far as possible on the Royal Courts—it clearly knows of the Statute of Edward I just referred to, and in another case in 1409 when the defendants, who were duly summoned according to the custom of the manor, failed to appear, directions were given to take the land into the lord's hand, and in the margin is 'Cape Magnum', which was the writ used in the King's Courts for the King to take land into his hands, and if the tenant came not at the day given him thereby he lost his land. Did lawyers then practise in the Manor Court? When in 1378 William Kyng, in a plea of debt, is present by his attorney Roger Kantebery and denies the debt, it is possible that Kantebery, a name which does not appear among the tenants, was a professional lawyer. In 1407 there is a plea of debt in which Richard Langhurst claims from John Frank 3*s*. for a writ (pro brevi) and other things bought from him with damages 12*d*. But in any case all representatives in Court certainly were not lawyers, for in some cases, e.g. when Constance Lovelane in a plea of land in 1404 puts John Bradewell in her place to win or lose, or Alice Tygge puts John Clerk similarly in 1408, the names of the representatives appear to be those of tenants. In the great majority of cases litigants evidently had to conduct their cases in person, or perhaps for that reason failed to appear.

The cases other than land cases fall into a few clearly defined classes. The most numerous are pleas of Trespass, of which some fifty are recorded, many, however, ending in the plaintiff being fined for failing to appear. Animals were, of course, a fertile source of quarrel. Thus, Thomas Brygger in 1378 proceeds against John atte Pende because his dogs have torn and bitten plaintiff's pigs in the highway and elsewhere, to the damage of the said Thomas of 12*d*., and John Frank claims 20*d*.

damages against Richard Brugger in 1408 because his dog killed a ewe worth 12*d*. John Bradewell's dog must have had a peculiarly bad reputation, for in 1409 John Cotes alleged that the animal broke into his house and ate up meat to the loss of the said John Cotes which he put at 10*s*. Bradewell, it is hardly necessary to say, contended that he had no dog which behaved in this way, and this he offered to verify by making his law.[1]

William Joye v. William Kyng, in 1410, is a case of a different kind. Here the plaintiff contended that Kyng had ploughed half an acre at Longlandes belonging to plaintiff and trampled and used his grass, and the damage he put at 3*s*. 4*d*. Kyng denies and alleges that the half-acre was his own. The homage inquire and find that the land is Joye's, and that he should recover his damages, which, however, they assess at only 4*d*. And Kyng has to pay his 2*d*. Now this case is interesting because it seems to show that whatever the law you could in fact establish a title to land by means of a plea of trespass. For the Court Roll never in those days defined the boundaries of tenements, and when Kyng alienated or died his successor would presumably have only been admitted to whatever Kyng in fact held—the title would be to 'the tenement late William Kyng's'.

In 1406 a batch of fourteen cases of trespass was compromised. The trespasses were all against John Clerk, excepting the last, which was against John Fyssher. Unfortunately the exact subject of dispute does not appear.

The next most numerous class is pleas of Debt, which do not number quite half those of Trespass. They are for barley worth 3*s*. or two bushels of malt, or for 8*d*. for the hire of a house, or 2*s*. for the rent of a croft of land and damages 12*d*., or for sums

[1] Bradewell appears to have been a troublesome fellow. In 1409 he was park-keeper and swore that John Cotes and others had hunted rabbits in the lord's warren, and they admitted this and were fined, so Cotes's action was probably inspired by revenge. But the next entry shows that Bradewell had to find pledges for carrying out the injunctions of the lord and tenants, his mainpernors being put under penalty of losing their tenements, and the bedel was to arrest his goods. What the meaning of this was does not appear, but it is certain that Bradewell was convicted before the Justices of the King's Bench of a trespass done with force and arms on Arundell and was outlawed, for after Arundell's death he obtained a pardon (Calendar of Patent Rolls, 20 Nov. 1423).

of money lent, as 10*s.* 7½*d.* and 12*d.* damages, or 3*s.* 4*d.* and 12*d.* damages. It must be remembered that a direct claim for interest on money was not permissible, and such claims had to be made in the shape of claims for damage.

There are a very few pleas of Contract; e.g. in 1378 Richard atte Hyde claims to have sold 100 cartloads of marl to Richard Bromman for 16*s.* 8*d.*, of which 8*s.* 4*d.* had been paid.

In 1411 there is a plea of waste, in which John Wythemere sues Richard Munday for waste in respect of 100 plum trees and 20 ashes in a half-virgate called Godards, which Munday held for life with reversion to Wythemere.

In 1409 John Tygge was fined 2*d.* for failing to answer Alice Tygge about the execution of the will of John Tygge, senior.

The foregoing summary will give an idea of the civil business of the Court. The outstanding feature is the litigiousness of the tenants. When Wythemere was suing Munday for waste in the case just referred to, Munday was trying to get even with him by starting two pleas of debt, a plea of contract, and a plea of trespass. One of the pleas of debt broke down at once as Munday failed to pursue it and was fined 2*d.* When Brygger was recovering from atte Pende for damage done to his pigs in 1378, atte Pende was bringing two pleas of trespass against him, one of which he won and the other he lost.

Nor was litigation in the Tygge family confined to the case just referred to. Alice brought two pleas of debt against John, in one of which she claimed to have lent him 3*s.* 4*d.* with 12*d.* damages—this case she won. The other she failed to pursue and had to pay the customary 2*d.* The year before she had brought a plea of trespass against him for entering and carrying off her corn and put her loss at 10*s.*; John admitted, but asked to be assessed by the homage, who put the loss at three bushels of corn. And in another case he had been fined 2*d.* for unjustly detaining part of her dower.[1]

[1] Peasant proprietors are commonly litigious. Certainly the tenants of Carshalton were so in 1361 (see Carshalton Court Rolls printed by the Surrey Record Society, p. 15). The Tooting Beck Court Rolls of these two reigns show outbursts of litigation, e.g. five pleas of trespass in Oct. 1402 all part of a quarrel between Robert Crafte and Richard Bradwatere and five cases in Oct. 1409 in three of which Richard Bradwatere was also concerned.

A few words should be said as to the procedure followed in the Court. In the leet cases we are merely informed that a presentment is made, e.g. that the highway at Pokenyllyslonde is under water through the failure of John atte Wode to clear his ditches, therefore he is in mercy, and a fine of *2d.* is recorded; or that Peter atte Mere insulted Juliana Kyng and unjustly drew blood from her, therefore he is in mercy and a fine of *2d.* is recorded. But in the civil litigation the cases are recorded at much greater length. Let us take the exact record of the case about Bradwell's voracious dog (1409): 'John Cotes complains against John Bradewell in a plea of trespass. And he complains that on the 8th day of July in the ninth year of the present King the dog of the aforesaid John Bradewell broke into the house of the aforesaid John Cotes and ate his bread and meat there to the loss of the aforesaid John Cotes of 10*s.*, &c. And the aforesaid John Bradewell says that he had no dog who made such trespass on the aforesaid John as he in his count alleges. And this he offers to verify by law &c. And he has a day to make his law by the next Court.'

This is clearly a record in a fixed form, since it is so familiar that it is abbreviated by &c. The &c. covered e.g. the plaintiff's production of suit (i.e. witness to show a prima facie case), which, though indispensable, was now a mere formality. The form is modelled on the practice of the King's Courts, though in allowing wager of law in trespass it seems to have been behind them.[1] The wager of law consisted merely in bringing a varying number of persons—there are cases in these rolls of three or four, or even twelve, including the defendant—to swear to the defendant's case. They were not witnesses in the modern sense, i.e. persons who had personal knowledge of the facts in issue, who would say what they knew and be examined on their evidence. They were a survival of an earlier age, when the parties appeared with their supporters, and the Court did little more than keep the peace between them, or settle how (e.g. by battle) they should fight it out. The system seems to us absurd, but in the Manor Court, where every one knew everybody, it must have been easier to assess the value of the oaths of the compurgators than it could be in a modern court. The Court in

[1] See Holdsworth, i. 307.

fixing the number of compurgators no doubt considered the credibility of the defendant. When Thomas Whyte in 1406 claimed 1*s*. 6*d*. for fencing 18 perches and 3*s*. 4*d*. damages from John Sutton, we may suppose that Sutton's character for truthfulness stood low, for he was told to bring eleven compurgators. Nor, it seems, was the wager invariably accepted, for in 1405 John Frank proceeded against John Wyker and his wife in a plea of trespass. The latter waged their law that they were in no respect guilty. They were summoned and appeared, but the decision was that Frank should recover damages, though he only got 4*s*. out of the 20*s*. which he claimed. Wager of law was not used in all pleas of trespass, but it was the ordinary procedure in pleas of debt.

An alternative method is that followed, e.g. in a case of trespass in 1408, in which John Frank complained that Richard Brugger's dog had killed one of his ewes. In this case the defendant, who denied the fact, puts himself on the homage, and Frank likewise. And thereupon the homage have a day to advise by the next Court and the parties to hear. Similarly in Joye v. Kyng, already referred to (1410), where Kyng was said to have ploughed Joye's land, defendant asks that inquiry may be made by the homage. And the same is sometimes done even in cases of debt, e.g. when Thomas Cook claims 2*s*. rent and 12*d*. damages from Gilbert Whyte (1405). This is the earliest case on the roll of a plea of debt in which law was not waged.

To leave the matter to the homage to decide out of court would not seem to us a satisfactory method, but it at least has the merit of allowing inquiry. The homage were acquainted with the facts, or in the position to make themselves acquainted, and as compared with wager of law it is a step towards deciding the case on the merits. If we may judge from the readiness of the Banstead tenants to resort to the Court to settle their quarrels, we may conclude that whatever the defects of the system they did not regard the Court as unwilling or unable to do justice among themselves.

IV

THE BANSTEAD COURT ROLL IN THE REIGNS OF HENRY V AND HENRY VI

SEVENTY-SEVEN Courts in all with twelve Views are preserved between the accession of Henry V in March 1413 and July 1433, after which the roll is lost till 1486. In the reign of Henry V the roll runs to the end of 1417, after which there is one Court in 1418 and four Courts with a View in 1421. In the reign of Henry VI the roll runs from the View of 1422 to April 1425, and again from January 1430 to July 1433; there is only one Court in 1426, two in 1427, one in 1428, and none in 1429.[1]

The Court was particularly active in 1415, 1416, and 1417, in each of which years seven Courts and a View were held, and similar activity was shown in 1430 and in 1432, in which last year eight Courts and a View were held.

The entries on the roll do not, of course, differ greatly in character from those in the reigns of Richard II and Henry IV, which formed the subject of the last chapter. The most interesting point is the continuation of the struggle between Sir Richard Arundel and the tenants. Arundel was a man of influence entrusted by the King with important positions such as the custody of Bamborough Castle and Rochester Castle,[2] and the tenants, apparently convinced that they were not themselves strong enough to resist him, appealed directly to the King in a Petition which is preserved in the Record Office.[3]

[1] The Courts of 22 Dec. 1414 and 29 July 1433 (the last before the break) are printed in full in the Appendix.

[2] Information with regard to him will be found in Collectanea Topographica et genealogica, vi. 1–20, and some of it is also given in Hutchins's History of Dorset (1868), iii. 475, under Wichampton, which Arundel held.

[3] Ancient Petitions, File 92, No. 4576. The full text is printed in i. 150–3. The Petition, which is damaged, has unfortunately no date, but is addressed to Henry V and treats Arundel as living. Arundel died 3 June 1419 (see I.P.M. taken at Rochester 22 Nov. 7 H. V. Exchequer Series, 1–117/11). As the fine of 40*s*. referred to seems to be that inflicted at the Court of December 1414 and there was an agreement over the election of bedel in April 1415 and some sort of settlement over the fugitive bondmen seems to have been reached in July 1416, the Petition may be tentatively dated early in 1415.

The complaints made by the tenants were as follows:

(1) New charges contrary to their customary tenure had been imposed, which were driving tenants out of the manor.

(2) In particular John Colcok, Richard Colcok, John Wythemere and John Clerk are mentioned as having resisted and being threatened with the loss of their lands.

(3) The tenants were fined IX marks (£6) for resisting the new impositions, and because the sum of 26*s.* 8*d.* was in arrear John White was imprisoned in Arundel's house in London till he could get surety.

(4) Arundel took Robert and Peter atte Mere and imprisoned them at Banstead as bondmen, though they and all other tenants were, and their ancestors had been, free time out of mind, and amerced them excessively from Court to Court to the sum of 40*s.*, and for these amercements distrained their cattle.

(5) He claimed Juliana Lampit, who had been a free tenant of the manor for over sixty years, to be his bondwoman, and imprisoned her till she paid £5.

(6) He made tenants Bedels against the tenure of their holdings, and claimed them to be bondmen, and fined them.

(7) John Taillour, Richard Colcok and John Clerk, old tenants, have left the manor, and many more intend to leave unless their wrongs are remedied.

(8) The tenants are distrained by the King's Bailiff for Arundel's arrears due to the Exchequer (to which he had to pay any surplus over 80 marks received from Banstead, Walton, and Charlwood granted to him for life), and they are put to great inconvenience and loss.

No reply to this petition appears to have been preserved.

How far do the manor rolls sustain these complaints, and what was the result?

We have seen that already according to the Court Roll in 1412, Robert atte Mere the lord's bondman and all the bond homage had been fined for failing to produce William Bode and other fugitive bondmen, to which it may be added that Robert atte Mere was probably an obstinate fellow, for in the same year it is recorded that he, the lord's bondman and bedel of the manor, though enjoined by the lord through the Park-keeper to carry a buck to London declined to do so, and showed contempt for the lord's directions. Similar entries of fines occur in 1413, 1414, 1415, and in the earlier part of 1416, except that in July 1414 Peter atte Mere takes the place of Robert. The amount of the fines, however, rises. 40*d.* is regularly imposed until December 1415, when the amount rises to 6*s.* 8*d.*, and for ten successive Courts that amount is recorded. But in June 1416 the fine drops to 3*s.* 4*d.*, and in July it is recorded that Peter atte Mere and the whole bond homage having again failed to produce William Bode and the lord's other fugitive bondmen, Peter says that he is not a bondman, and entirely denies that he is bound to carry out the order, so it is necessary to consult with the lord. At the next Court there is again an entry that Peter atte Mere and the whole bond homage have a day to produce the fugitives, but there is no fine. No settlement of this question is recorded on the rolls, but it would appear that the claim was in fact dropped. It is clear, however, that Arundel or his steward did not abandon the right, for in May 1421 when Arundel was dead and his widow held the manor for her life, there is an entry that further directions were given to seize (seisire) Agatha Willy, daughter of Henry Willy the lady's bondman (nativi domine), and this reappears at three following courts. There was a tenant named Henry Willy who was paying chevage in 1368 for having licence to remain outside the domain of our lady the Queen[1] (who then held the manor), and the woman apparently lived at Wallington, for Agatha Willy in 1415 was presented by Henry Willy, tithing-man there, and fined for breaking the assize of ale. No result seems to have followed from the order.

But there are two cases on the roll which show that on occasion the right to levy chevage was still enforced. In July 1426 Peter Carter, the lord's bondman,[2] paid 6*d.* to enable him to remain outside the lordship for a year, and in April 1428 it is recorded that Carter has left the lordship and is at Croydon, and he is to be produced at the next Court under a penalty of 6*s.* 8*d.* Some of the Carters were apparently well-to-do, for in 1432 the heir of Joan Carter who held by

[1] See i. 120.

[2] *Nativus domini.* Lady Arundel held the manor, but the clerk probably wrote domini from force of habit.

copy (per copiam curie) according to the custom of the manor two tofts and 6½ acres was John Carter, citizen and dyer of London, and it is reasonable to suppose that Peter Carter had special reasons for paying his chevage.

The other case is that of Robert atte Mere. In December 1430 directions are given to the bond homage to produce him at the next Court under penalty of 3*s*. 4*d*. He has left the lordship without licence. In April 1431 he puts himself on the lord's mercy for leaving the lordship without leave. There is no fine, but the matter was to be further considered (the record is damaged). Probably Robert wanted to get his land back, but in December William atte Wode, tyler, took certain lands and tenements which formerly belonged to Robert atte Mere, the lord's bondman, which had long been in the lord's hands for lack of a tenant. And William and his son had seisin for the term of their lives, and of the survivor of them to hold by the rod according to the custom of the manor for the rents and services due and customary. And they paid for fine 20*s*. So it would seem that in this case the tenant was defeated, and the lord not only succeeded in evicting him, but obtained a new tenant on terms which secured to himself a reversion of the property to which he would otherwise never have been entitled.

These facts point to the conclusion that at Banstead between 1413 and 1433 the lord did not succeed in enforcing the obligations of bondmen generally and latterly rarely attempted to do so, but that he never abandoned his rights, and when a tenant's necessities enabled him to do so, he enforced them.

Another standing subject of dispute between lord and tenants besides the removal of bondmen was the election of bedel. This office, as remarked in the last chapter, was no sinecure, and involved considerable liabilities since the bedel was himself liable to fine if he failed to distrain to the satisfaction of the Court. Thus in October 1413 he was fined 12*d*. for failing properly to distrain the tenants of the Manor of Chaldon to satisfy the lord for several defaults of suit of Court, and 6*d*. for a similar failure to distrain the feoffees of the lands and tenements of Thomas Berwe, and at the next Court in December he was fined 6*d*. in each case. At the court of February 1414,

Thomas Berwe appeared, but the bedel was again fined 12*d.* in the Chaldon case, and 4*d.* in April, and 2*d.* in July and October. In December and the following Courts he was fined nothing, though the Chaldon tenants still made default, perhaps because he could pay nothing. Finally, Sir John Wyltechyre appeared in April and agreed with the lord for the aforesaid defaults paying 8*d.*, which would appear to show that it was cheaper to default than to fail to distrain the defaulter to the steward's satisfaction.

In May 1413 it is recorded that the homage elected John White of Banstead and Robert atte Mere to the office of bedel, and John was sworn, but in October, when directions were given to the whole homage to elect a bedel as was the habit according to the custom of the manor, they refused the said election and were fined 20*s.*[1] No explanation is given, but in September the death of John Whyte junior, who may be the same man, was presented (the name is common in the roll). In December orders are given to seize into the lord's hands all the lands and tenements of John Colcok, John Clerk, and Richard Colcok, because they refuse to elect a bedel. In February 1414 a similar order is made for the same reason with regard to the lands of Arnold Lovelane, John Herward and John Wythemere. Fines of 6*s.* 8*d.* are imposed on the homage in April and July, of 20*s.* in October, and of 40*s.* in December. But in January 1415 it is recorded that the homage of Banstead still refuses to elect a bedel as by law and custom they should do, and that it was therefore necessary to consult with the lord, and in April the roll recites the objection of the tenants to elect, who said that 'it is not the tenure of their lands to do that office as they are ordered', and records that an agreement was made with the lord. The conditions however are not recorded, and the agreement did not end the struggle, but though the tenants' continued refusal to elect is recorded (May and December 1415 and October 1416) there are no more fines. It would appear, therefore, that on the main issue the tenants won.

[1] At the View on the same date the Banstead homage elected Thomas at Wode as Constable, and he was sworn, but this was clearly a different office.

But though the lord could not force them to elect a bedel he retained the lands of several tenants. In April 1415 at the same Court as that at which the agreement is recorded it is also recorded that all the lands and tenements of Arnold Lovelane, John Wethemere, John Herwarde, John Colcok, and Richard Colcok remain in the lord's hands. In December 1415, Arnold Lovelane surrendered 12 acres called Heldelond, a copse, a toft with the engaging name of Pekehoggeshawe, and three other pieces of land amounting in all to 6½ acres to the use of Richard Colcok, on which no heriot fell due as he remains a tenant. And Richard was admitted to hold by the usual rents and services, and paid a fine of 2*s*. But in the margin is the note 'It is revoked because it was seized before into the lord's hands. Therefore the fine is void'. So it would appear that the conveyance was not carried through.

In March 1416, however, two of the men mentioned were quarrelling in circumstances which indicate that they both in fact held land, for John Wethemere claimed 10*s*. in a plea of trespass against John Herwarde for entering his garden at Banstead with his sheep and eating and trampling down the growing grass. Herwarde admitted the facts, but disputed the amount of the damage. In April 1416 John Kyng, carpenter, surrenders land of which one rood is described as lying between the land of Arnold Lovelane on the south and certain other land, and one rood between the land of John Herward on the south, and of Richard Colcok on the north, to the use of Richard Colcok junior, who is admitted to hold by the customary services, and pays a fine of 12*d*.; and in 1421 John Withemere conveys 2½ acres to Robert Stretton, clerk, without any objection being indicated.

It would seem, therefore, that though the roll contains no statement that they regained possession of their lands, at least some of them in fact did so. They were, however, still exposed to trouble. In June 1416 it was presented that John Colcok senior, who held certain lands and tenements by the rod according to the custom of the manor, is dead, and Richard Colcok junior is his heir as younger son. He asked to be admitted, but because at the Court held in December 1413 all the said lands and tenements were seized into the lord's hands, and are so seized (et sic seisita existant) the lord must be consulted and the admission is deferred. In January 1417 Richard has a day for being admitted, and he may have got his land back, but it is not clear what was the position of land seized into the lord's hand and never apparently released formally even if it was, in fact, reoccupied. No doubt the steward used any opportunity offered by the anomalous position to squeeze a tenant.

An entry at the Court of March 1431 seems to show that despite the agreement the old claim about the appointment of bedel was still maintained, for it is recorded that the homage had a day to elect a bedel to collect the lord's rents and do other services under a penalty of 100*s*. But the next court merely shows that they still had a day, and there is in the existing rolls no evidence that any fine was ever inflicted. The entry, therefore, looks like a bit of bluff, the more so that in 1432 the bedel was John Wethemere. Probably terms were arranged. John Wethemere when he became bedel had his troubles with his former allies, for Richard Colcok in August made a rescue of two horses, and in October of cattle, which had been seized and impounded by the bedel on behalf of the lord. This cost Colcok at the Court in December no less a fine than 10*s*., and smaller fines were inflicted on two other tenants.

The Rolls throw no light on Arundel's alleged illegal imprisonment of tenants—such cases were not unknown in the fifteenth century[1]—but they do throw some light on the grounds for the lord's claims. The atte Mere family had certainly been accustomed to serve as bedels, for in 1363 John ate Mer was bedel, and in 1393 after a reference to (? another) John atte Mere as having acted as bedel there is the following entry with 'of Bedels' in the margin (there is an erasure in the document). 'John atte Mere and Thomas atte Mere, and the lord chose one of them according to the custom of the manor, namely John atte Mere.' And merchet had been paid on atte Mere marriages[2] in 1408.

[1] e.g. a petition of 1404 alleges that good and honest burgesses and free tenants are imprisoned till they make fine and ransom or consent to hold their lands in villenage. (Quoted by Holdsworth, History of English Law, iii. 503, who gives other instances.)

[2] See p. 22.

Juliana Lampit, who according to the tenants had been a free tenant of the manor for over sixty years but was claimed by the lord as a bondwoman, was evidently the woman who, described as the widow of Ralph Lamputte, in 1401 surrendered a cottage and 7 acres to the use of John Hereward and Mabel his wife, her daughter. In 1377 Ralph Lampytt, no doubt her husband, had been doing carting for the repairs to the Lodge at Banstead Park for 8*d*. a day.[1] The name is common in the Banstead documents between 1325 and 1433, after which it disappears.[2] In 1325 William Lomputte had held one farthing land and a half of 7 acres, and he was liable for hoeing and ploughing at boon days, and taking out dung, and doing various other villein services. In 1402 John Lamputte junior and John Lamputte senior were to be distrained to answer for the defects of their 'bond tenements', and in 1413 John Lomput junior acknowledged that he held from the lord 4 acres of the half virgate called Joyners land which formerly belonged to Robert Cole. Now Robert Cole in 1369 was certainly paying chevage[3], a sure mark of villein status, and the purpose of the record probably was to make Lamput's status clear.

Members of all the families referred to in the petition, atte Mere, Lamputs, Colcoks, Clerks, Wythemeres, Taillours, held in villenage, and from the tenure to the status was in law an easy step. For however much economic and social changes might be altering the position of the villein, however much the Royal Courts might lean in favour of freedom, the legal status of villenage was still untouched.[4]

There is no evidence on the rolls of the truth of the complaint about distresses by the King's bailiff for Arundel's debts, and

[1] i. 134.

[2] Unless we identify it with Lambert, but the identification seems wrong. Lampit, Lamputte, or atte Lamputte (i. 89), Lampytte, Lomputte, Lomput, Lompit, (Lomput being probably the commonest form) seem to mean Loam pit, i.e. it is a local name like Green, Wood, or Lane, whereas Lambert with its variants Lambyrd and Lambard, none of which occur at Banstead before 1500, is evidently a surname formed from a Christian name.

[3] i. 120.

[4] It survived in a decadent condition all through the Tudor period, and was never legally abolished. The last case was tried in 1618 (Holdsworth, History of English Law, iii. 491–508).

indeed on 14 January 1413 Arundel had a pardon of all debts, accounts, arrears, &c., both in the time of Richard II and from the time of the coronation of Henry IV,[1] but it is, of course, possible that he was hard up for money. On October 1413 the steward, in the case of an ordinary succession to three farthing lands formerly William Kyng's, imposed a fine which the mother of the grandchild, who was the heir, declined to pay. The amount is not stated, but in July 1414 she paid 13*s*. 4*d*. for the custody of the lands and guardianship. The fact that at the Court in September it is recorded that a horse valued at 12*s*. was taken as the heriot on Kyng's death, but that he had, as it is said, a better animal, and orders were given to seize another one, certainly looks as if pressure was being put on to extract as much as possible.

On the other hand, the tenants were very troublesome about performing their obligations. The Rolls are full of directions to repair tenements which the tenants were very slow to execute. It was presented in December 1413 that the tenement of John Lomputte junior called Hugons is ruinous, and in January 1416 he is still being required to repair it. Possibly he found his duties as ale-taster too absorbing. In any case he regularly paid a fine of 2*d*. till the penalty threatened was raised, when he evidently preferred to do the necessary repairs. There was endless trouble about fencing round the manor and repairing the grange. In March 1416 the homage was fined 20*d*. for not repairing the fence, and in July they were required to certify whose obligation it was to repair. In July 1421 it is specially recorded that the Vicar (who is fined) has been bound from time beyond the memory of man to repair the fence round the manor on the east of the churchyard. In March 1424 it is recorded that there must be a conference with the lady's counsel (cum consilio domine) about the repair of the grange which the tenants are bound to repair by their tenure as appears by the custumal.[2] In 1425 John Colcok senior, Thomas Hunt, William Joye, and John Taillour were required to produce

[1] See Calendar of Patent Rolls.

[2] Presumably the Extent of 1325 printed in vol. i. See especially p. 71, where Richard Kyriel, a typical customary tenant, 'will help in the repair of the grange as is proper'.

proof of their claim to be exempt from the repairs of the lady of the manor, that is in roofing. As over each name is written 'Cogn.' it is pretty clear that when pressed they abandoned the claim. Almost the last entry which appears on the roll in July 1433 is an injunction to all the tenants both of Banstead and of the Weald, who by reason of their customary tenure are bound to repair the grange and fence round the manor to do the necessary work. The payment of ½*d.* for pigs (avisagium) shows a strong tendency to drop, and the roll closes with directions so far not complied with to certify the names of tenants who should pay this due. There are, of course, cases of poaching, and in 1430 the Vicar lopped the lord's trees in the fence between the manor and the churchyard (that is on the east side of the churchyard) and dug on the lord's ground a deep and dangerous well (profundum et periculosum). The tenement called Watts had to be seized into the lord's hands for the waste both in regard to trees and buildings which the tenant had done, as was recorded when a new tenant was admitted (1426). Some of the buildings had apparently fallen down. In 1432 John Cherlewode appropriated for the purpose of enclosure two perches of the lord's land at Normere. And so on. We may safely conclude that all the grievances were not on one side.

The business transacted is of the same character as in the two previous reigns. There are usually nine tithings paying Borghsilver at the Views, viz. Banstead (three), Copthill, Hyde, Leigh, Sidlow Mill, Tadworth, and Wallington, but sometimes Leangre and Chalvedon (Chaldon) appear separately, and before 1417 Banstead has four tithings. The borghsilver at 1*d.* a head varied from year to year, being as high as 63*d.* in 1417, and down to 52*d.* in 1430, but the number both of tithings and of men in the tithings has clearly fallen since 1378, and the latter still more since 1325, when there were, in addition to 10 free tenants, 78 tenants in villenage in Banstead, and 26 in the Weald. If we add to the men in tithing represented by the borghsilver the tithing-men who did not themselves pay[1] we get a figure of 68 for 1432. The men capable of bearing arms (that is from 15 to 55 years of age)

[1] See p. 18.

in a modern European community are about one-quarter of the whole population, and even if we multiply by four we still do not get 300. But it would probably be much more correct to multiply by three, for the expectation of life in the fifteenth century was low, and there must have been much fewer men over 55 than now, and at the other end more boys were being put into the tithing. For instance it appears from the View of October 1415, that William Upton and John Colcok were sworn in to their tithing at Tadworth at the age of 12, and there was apparently no age limit at the other end. If, then, we multiply by three, we get a population of rather over 200. But to this figure must be added the free tenants and their servants.

The Views, which were held once a year, generally about Michaelmas (in 1426 for some reason the View was held in July), are mostly very formal affairs concerned with payment of borghsilver, filling up the tithings, presentation of nuisances, as that the footpath at Southmere leading from the tenement lately William Kyng's to the Church of Banstead is blocked by the neglect of Thomas Puplet, who is fined *2d.* (1416), breaches of the assize of ale, or small criminal cases as that Margaret, daughter of John Wethemere, entered the house of John Lovelane and wrongly took 1 kerchief, 1 wedding ring, and 1 'gambon de bacon', for which at the next ordinary Court—the case was not dealt with at a View—she was fined *2s.* (1424). But in 1415 there was more business than usual, and the twelve jurors declared on oath that a certain stranger with a certain woman came into the lordship and stayed there with various goods described, and he was pursued by Thomas atte Wode, the Constable, for suspected felony, but fled, and his goods remained in the custody of the Constable, and are valued for the lord by the tenants, viz. two old linen garments[1] price *2s.*, one cloak of dark red colour and two hoods (or caps) *4s.*, one coverlet *18d.*, one napkin and a towel *6d.*, and one sword *2s.* They also said that William Swanlond, chaplain, was harboured within the manor and stayed for a quarter of a year and more. And he fled for reasons unknown. And the Constable seized his goods, and they are valued as follows:

[1] Lintheamina, which may mean linen cloths.

1 wallet price *2d.*, 2 hammers with two 'graffing sawes' *8d.*, 4 chisels, and so forth—it rather looks as if the chaplain was after all nothing but an honest workman, except that near the end of the list is 'one old book valued at *6d*'. But as there was no special reason why the goods of William Swanlond should fall to the lord better inquiry was to be made. And as no more appears on the roll, it may be that Swanlond returned and made good his claim to his goods.

The Views always close with a solemn statement that the twelve jurors whose names are given[1] say on their oath that the tithing-men and ale-taster have made true presentments and concealed nothing, or that some one has failed to do so. The jurors are called 'Duodecim liberi juratores' in the roll of Henry VI, and in 1402, 1406, and 1414 there is 'xij liberi' in the text or margin. They had indeed been called 'duodecim liberi juratores' in 1378. But from 1415 to 1422 they are merely called 'Duodecim juratores'—possibly an echo of the struggle over the question of status, for the jurors include the names of members of families concerned in that struggle.

The business of the Court (curia or parva curia) continues, of course, to be largely concerned with transfers of land. The formula 'to hold according to the custom of the manor for the due and customary services' which had been in use since the accession of Henry IV[2] is well established. But tenants could not always be found on the customary terms, and e.g. at the Court of February 1414 there is a record of four parcels of land let for money rents (ad firmam) of from *16d.* to *6s. 8d.* a year, of a wood for *8d.*, and of a mill at Kersalton for *9s.*

There are, too, a number of cases of tenants obtaining the lord's licence to let for a term of years, e.g. in 1417 Thomas Hunt and Avis his wife let to John Wethemere 12 acres lying

[1] In 1415 they are called 'infrascripti', but the names are in fact not given. In 1414 there are only nine names, though the margin has 'xij liberi'.

[2] The formula in the rolls of Richard II is somewhat different, e.g. 'Habendum et tenendum predicto Rogero et sequele sue reddendo et faciendo redditus servicia et consuetudines' (1383), which it will be observed only speaks of consuetudines as obligations, whereas 'according to the custom of the manor' may imply rights as well as obligations. The Tadworth Roll, however, already in 1394 (see p. 48) uses 'secundum consuetudinem manerii per servicia inde debita et consueta'.

in different parcels in the fields of Banstead for 9 years, at a rent of 8*s*. 6*d*. The lessors, who pay 12*d*. for the licence, will bear during the aforesaid term all the burdens due to the chief lord of the fee. Similar provision occurs in a lease in the same year by Alice Coumbe, of Takeles, to Thomas Hayton, for 7 years at a rent of 13*s*. 4*d*. But in a lease in 1416 by John Chuk to John Clerk of Crocherestenement, for 3 years at a rent of 3*s*. 4*d*. Clerk undertakes the obligations due to the lord. It is not clear why in this case the tenant took the obligation. When in October 1423 Thomas Hunt gets a licence at the cost of 6*d*. to let Thomas atte Wode 10 acres lying separately in the fields of Banstead for 6 years at a rent of 7*s*. 4*d*. nothing is said of the burdens due to the lord, nor is anything said in two other similar cases at the same Court.

All these leases, whether of lord to tenant or of tenant to tenant, are obviously inconsistent with the old manorial economy, and a lease for a money payment from lord to tenant is fundamentally inconsistent with the conception of villein status. We have not, however, yet reached the stage when the Royal Courts, which leant heavily against villein status, had laid down, as they did in 1496, that a lease for years by the lord to a villein operated like the feoffment of a freehold interest, as an enfranchisement.[1] Indeed, had this been the law, no petition of the tenants to Henry V would have been necessary, for already in 1354 the lord was leasing land for a term of years to tenants.[2]

It had always been usual to require new occupants of land to show by what title they held. The use of copies had now become so common that when in 1427 John Kyng, who held half a virgate, died, and they said that his wife Juliana held jointly with him, the order of the Court runs to distrain the said Juliana to show her copy (ad ostendendum copiam).

At the Court of July 1426 is recorded a surrender out of Court, a surrender made by John Brustowe to Thomas Lechford, the lord's tenant, in the presence of John Wilshire, Robert Brustowe, and other tenants of the lord. These were substantial people, and the heriot was a cow worth 8*s*., and the

[1] Holdsworth, iii. 501.

[2] See p. 16, also i. 93.

fine was 20*s.*, so the form, which is common enough later, may have been a concession to influential tenants.

It will be remembered that in 1408 the Prior of Southwark was required to produce his title deeds to a parcel of land called Collinsland.[1] The roll is not complete, and it is not clear whether the Prior took any action at that time. But at the Court of December 1414 it was presented that the Prior of St. Mary de Overee in Suthwerk holds a parcel of land called Colyneslonde by what title is unknown, and he is required to produce it. The Convent at this time held the advowson of Banstead, and had done so since the time of Henry I, and it is not clear why the question was raised. The Prior, in any case, was in no hurry to answer it, and it was only after he had been distrained in 100 sheep and his pledges had been twice fined that he appeared by his attorney Walter Hook in July 1416, and produced three deeds, one an undated grant by Robert de Berewe and Matilda his wife, and the other two grants (one dated 15 February 1269) by Sir John de Burgh, (the son of the Great Justiciar) who subsequently sold the manor to Edward I. The land was, of course, held in free alms. After the first two deeds there is a note to consult with the lord, but not after the last. If it is permissible to hazard a guess to explain what seems to be the strange proceeding of so persistently questioning so long established a title, and the steady disregard of the process of the Court by the Prior, it may be suggested that the tenants in villenage at Banstead hoped to find in the documents some flaw in the Prior's right to exact services. The second document (that of 1269) quit-claimed to the Prior and Convent all suit of Court, rents of 7*s.* 6*d.*, customs . . . aids in harvest (the document is damaged here), to wit of four men. As the question does not reappear on the roll, it was presumably settled, whatever it was.

There is one case of an attempt to enforce the Statute of Labourers, for it is recorded at the Court held in April 1413 (not, as might have been supposed proper, at a View) that the bedel had had orders to compel Stephen Wyke, labourer, with others to appear at the Court before the steward to take the

[1] Ostendendi evidencias. See p. 19. Collinslands still appear on the Tithe map just south of Great Dicelands on the Reigate Road.

oath to serve in husbandry according to the form of the Statute. But Wyke did not appear, but removed himself, and was accordingly fined *2d.*, a decision which, as he was no longer within the jurisdiction, he no doubt treated with contempt.

The contentious business of the Court does not differ greatly from that in the two previous reigns. The most numerous cases are pleas of land, and of the rest most are pleas of trespass, e.g. for damage done by sheep or pigs to crops, or for cutting down a tree. There are half-a-dozen pleas of debt. The case of Rokynham v. Lovelane, decided in October 1423, is worth noting. The claim was for 5*s.* for a quarter of malt bought at Whitsuntide. Defendant denied, and put himself to his law (ponit se ad legem), on which he was given a day to make his law six handed. Compurgation was going out of favour in the Royal Courts, but it still lingered in actions for debt (and indeed was not finally abolished till 1833).[1] It had, of course, a longer life in the manorial Courts than in the Royal Courts, but it is the only case of this date recorded at Banstead, the defendant usually putting himself on the homage.

There is one plea of contract (in 1431) the circumstances of which are sufficiently curious to be worth mentioning. Peter atte Mere claimed that John Mathewe, the Vicar of Banstead, had agreed with him that he should carry the Vicar's oats for a sum (which is left blank on the roll), and the Vicar was to hold him harmless against any one whatsoever. This, however, got Peter into trouble with the lord's bedel, who had seized the said oats for various fines incurred by the Vicar, and as the Vicar refused to see Peter through, he claimed 3*s.* 4*d.* The Vicar denied the agreement, and the matter was referred to the homage,[2] who, as Peter was fined *2d.*, evidently did not believe in the alleged indemnity. Nor, indeed, is it the least likely. The Vicar (who was the man who dug the dangerous well) must have known, and Peter probably did, that the oats were under arrest.

To complete the history it may be added that Lady Arundell

[1] Holdsworth's History of English Law, i. 305–8.

[2] The defendant 'ponit se super inquisitionem', and the plaintiff does the same, the margin having Homag'.

died on 2 August 1436, and at the inquisition held at Leatherhead on 26 October[1] the jurors found that she held the Manor of Banstead for life, 'in which Manor of Banstead there are £19 10s. 0d. of annual rent of tenants both free and bond' (tam liberorum tenentium quam nativorum). But, as already observed, the legal status of villenage was untouched. Nevertheless, it is interesting to note among the names of the jurors Richard Colcok and John Colcok.

[1] Exchequer, I.P.M., 15 Hen. VI, 161/15.

V

THE EARLIER COURT ROLLS OF TADWORTH AND PERROTTS

THE earliest Tadworth Court is that of Robert Wyndesore, Prior of Merton,[1] held on 1 June 1394, which is followed by two courts of 1395. No further Courts are preserved till 1462, when the series resumes, and is fairly continuous.

The Courts of 1 June 1394 and of 14 November 1462 are printed in full in the Appendix, and also a Rental of 1474.

In the Courts of Richard II, when surrenders and admissions occur, the formula used is 'To hold according to the custom of the manor for the services due and customary', a formula which was not used at Banstead till the following reign,[2] but the somewhat derogatory term 'sequela' is used, and the land is described as in bondagio or terra nativa. All these Courts have entries requiring the homage to bring back bondmen who have left the manor. The tenants according to the roll were tallaged yearly at the will of the lord, but as they paid 6*s*. at the first Court, and 6*s*. 8*d*. at each of the succeeding Courts, the payment was evidently, in fact, a fixed payment. There are the usual cases of tenants brought before the Court for trespass on the lord's pasture or wood, but there is only one case of litigation between tenants, viz. a plea of trespass relating to damage done by the defendant's pigs.

Note that as it is stated in the first Court that Thomas Gillem's homage was testified to by the farmer and others, it would appear that the Convent was leasing their manor.[3]

The Rental of 1474, which is defaced in places but is mostly legible,[4] was drawn up when John Kyngestone was Prior, and John Gysborne Cellarer. Kingston had been Prior since 1442 and died in 1485, when Gisborne succeeded him, living till 1502.[5] The Rental shows 6 free and 9 customary tenants. The

[1] Windsor, who had been a Canon of Merton, became Prior in 1368, and died in 1403. (Heales, Records of Merton Priory.)

[2] See p. 43.

[3] See i. 167.

[4] It is possible that the date should be 1475.

[5] Heales's Merton Priory.

latter have commuted nearly all their services for payments in money or kind, but they all still owe a little harvest labour. The basis of payment is 4*s*. per virgate with 2 cocks and 2 hens, and for labour remitted 6½ bushels of barley and 6½ bushels of oats, but with 2 days' labour remaining to be performed. The customary tenants are again described as owing tallage 'ad voluntatem domini'.

Both free and customary tenants pay castleguard for Rochester Castle. The origin of this is not clear, but in 1276 Westburgh (Great Burgh) was paying 12*s*. castleguard for Rochester, and South Tadworth came under a similar obligation, probably from having been held at one time with Chaldon.[1] In the Court of 28 May 1562 the payment is called 'Rochester rent'.

The latter Court is the first Court of Millicent Herrendenne, who was the widow of Edward Herrenden, who had bought the manor in 1553, and contains a statement of the tenants and their obligations at that date. The tenants, who are not distinguished as being free or customary, though their holdings are, of course, said to be held libere or per copiam, numbered 12 in all, which number was further reduced to 11 by the surrender at that Court by one tenant, Margarte Rytchebelle, widow, with her son of her tenement, part of Guyllamslond, to another tenant, Geoffrey Lamberd, who already held another part of Guyllamslond. The payments are similar to those in 1474 and the harvest labour is retained, e.g. Robert Moys, gentleman, who held by copy Odynges and other land was liable for 2½ days' work at harvest.

It is interesting to note, with reference to the names which occur in these Tadworth rolls, that the tithe map (see map at end of vol. i) shows the names Gillums field, Odens meadow, Watts field, Hidmans and Copley.

The Perrotts Court Rolls (which are in my own possession) are less interesting. They are not only much briefer, but nothing earlier than 1447 has survived. Only odd sheets have been preserved before 1639 when the roll begins to run regularly.

[1] See Chancery, I.P.M., 4 Edw. I, No. 19, on John de Bures. In 26 Edw. I, the I.P.M. (No. 24) on Roger de Covert shows that he owed 24*s*. for the same purpose. See also M. B. ii. 441.

The fifteenth-century Courts are reprinted in the Appendix. The entries all relate to Hamptons, which was subsequently known as Reads Rest. The Court of 1490 exists only in a paper copy, which was apparently made by John Lambert, then lord of the manor,[1] in 1603, when Philip Puplett was to be admitted, for there is a note which he seems to have put down for his own use to make clear the descent of the land.[2] The Courts of 1447 and 1461 are also recorded on parchments, both of which show signs of sewing.

[1] He had inherited Perrotts from his father in 1596, and sold it to his younger brother Edward in 1634, describing himself then as of Carshalton. He married Catherine, daughter of Philip Moys of Canons in Banstead.

[2] See p. 118.

VI

SOME OBSERVATIONS ON THE COURT ROLL IN TUDOR TIMES

WHEN the Banstead Court Roll resumes in 1486 the Views show little change. The tithing-men for Banstead, Tadworth, Copthill, Wallington, Chaldon, Leigh, and Sidlow Mill duly appear (or sometimes fail to appear), and present the common fine as before, and the usual presentments are made that ditches are not scoured, that a road is blocked or foundrous, that a horse or an ox has come as a stray, that certain tenants have made default of suit of Court, enrolments in the tithing are made, and fines are inflicted for small assaults, or on strangers who depastured their cattle on the common, the ale-taster is always active, and tithing-men and constables are elected. The Views tend to be jejune and stereotyped, but Tudor legislation occasionally threw new duties on them. Thus whereas in 1533 directions are merely given to repair certain highways under the usual penalty of a fine,[1] in 1581 we find that Richard Puplett failed with his cart in the repair of the highways for one day and George Richbell for two days 'contra formam statuti'. They are allowed time to do the work, but if they do not complete it, they will incur the penalty of the Statute.[2] Attempts are made to enforce the legislation which required the keeping of bows and arrows[3] and forbade unlawful games. Thus at the View of 7 October 1583 it was presented that John Johnson kept an ale-house and allowed men to play cards, backgammon (tabulis), and other unlawful games for one day contrary to the Statute, for which he forfeited 40*s.* (as provided by section vii of 33 Henry VIII, c. 9). But nearly all the presentments quoted later about the very important matter of depasturing sheep on the Downs were made at Courts, not at the Views.

The Court (or Court Baron, as it is called in Elizabeth's

[1] p. 100.

[2] p. 107. The Act of 5 Elizabeth, c. 13, had raised to six the number of days fixed by 2 & 3 Ph.&M., c. 8, at four.

[3] p. 107 and i. 277.

time[1]) grows longer and more detailed. In one respect it alters its character. It is no longer taken up with the continual litigation of the tenants among themselves. There are indeed some cases, e.g. at the Court of 7 March 1505 there are three pleas of trespass, all settled by agreement, and in 1583 Andrew Lambert brings a plea of caption and unjust detention of his sheep against William Atkinson and Ralph Trapps (in the course of which is set out the custom of the manor that customary tenements descend to the younger son), and another case with a plea of land follows. But it may be suspected that in these cases a special reason like the need for appealing to the Court Roll existed, and the tenants as a rule were either less litigious or fought out their quarrels elsewhere.

In its functions as a land registry, and more particularly one in which the lord had a pecuniary interest, the Court was very active. When the roll resumes it is full of directions to ascertain by what title a particular piece of land is held. For instance, at the Court of 23 April 1488 it is presented that Joan Parker now holds and occupies as free land a messuage and parcel of land in Horley, lately part of a virgate of land once William Vynersshe's, without title or estate, and without paying anything yearly to the lady of the manor, which land is held by copy of Court Roll. There are numerous cases in which it is recorded that tenants withheld the rent owing for years.[2] The activity of the Court in its inquiries into titles is, therefore, at least in part, explained by the attitude of the tenants.

The surrenders and admissions grow fuller and the land is more carefully described. The Court of 21 October 1533 printed in the Appendix well exemplifies this. At that Court, among other matters, the death of John Lambert, who had bought Perrotts and Well Farm in 1516, was presented, and

[1] See p. 105, which shows no trace of the distinction between a Court Baron and Customary Court suggested by Coke and Blackstone (Holdsworth, History of English Law, i. 182). The Court Baron is merely the Curia or parva Curia of earlier years; like them differentiated from the View, and though the Court is called a Court Baron in Lady Arundel's inquest in 1436 (p. 4) it is in fact not so called on the Court Roll till the first Court of Francis Carewe, Esqre., 23 March 1562. Even then, though the term Court Baron becomes usual, it is not always adhered to (e.g. in 15 Eliz. we get Curia again).

[2] For several cases see i. 157.

it will be seen that he died seized of a number of parcels of copyhold land which are all specified, and that his will and a deed relating to land in Horley are recited.[1] Nothing comparable to this elaborate entry exists in any of the pre-Tudor rolls, and indeed John Lambert's holding was of a somewhat different kind to anything which they show. Land held in villenage or copyhold land seems to have been transferred very freely in the Middle Ages, and often passed rapidly from family to family, of which a striking example will be found on the Tadworth rental of 1474, where William Mathew's customary virgate was once held by William Prophete, then by William Relff, then by Thomas Leangre, then by John Mathew.[2] The Tadworth rental also shows some signs of the agglomeration of copyholds. But John Lambert, who appears for the first time in Banstead in 1516, being then described as 'of Woodmansterne', where he had bought land in 1512, but of whom nothing is known earlier, and who appears on the subsidy roll of 1525 as paying far more for his goods than any one else on that list,[3] evidently set to work to build up an estate, and the land which he acquired in fact remained in the hands of his direct descendants until after the late war.

One of the main functions of the Court was to protect the interests of the lord and also of the tenants against encroachments. When the rolls resume, the wool of the sheep of Banstead Downs had already attained a high reputation,[4] and the rise in prices made sheep-farming very profitable. The temptation to neighbouring farmers who were not tenants of the manor to depasture their sheep on the Downs seems to have been irresistible. Already at the View of 17 April 1486 it is stated that John Cuddington of Cuddington and seven others of Cheam and Sutton are offending in this way, and a fine of 4*d.* is imposed on each. From 1516 onwards entries relating to

[1] The will is in Arch. Surrey, Heats 45. The copyhold lands in Banstead are there said to be insufficient to maintain the messuage in which he dwelt (Well Farm), which he left with the contents to his wife for life, and he therefore left her also an annuity of 40*s.* a year from Perrotts and Herrolds. The deed referred to was a mortgage by Robert Couper of copyhold lands in Horley for £40, which passed to Geoffrey, John's eldest son. Couper had evidently repaid the mortgage money, and is readmitted.

[2] p. 113. [3] i. 159. [4] See i. 17.

pasture on this common are very frequent, but become less so after the reign of Henry VIII, and after 1573 almost die out. At the Court of 15 October 1516 it was presented that John Codyngton, gentleman, was depasturing 800 sheep of his own or his tenants on Banstead Down, that John Legh, Knight, had 300 sheep there, John Puplett 300, and Thomas Compton 300. In 1521 and 1525 similar complaints were made of Cuddington and others, including William Kempsale of Kingswode, who had 600 sheep on the common called the Heth. Among other cases it was presented that three farmers of Cheam and five of Sutton were pasturing their sheep (no numbers are mentioned) on Banstead Down in 1555, but the trouble was by no means confined to encroachments by farmers in neighbouring parishes, for there was much difficulty with farmers in Banstead itself. At a Court of 23 October 1522 it was presented that Richard Moys, the farmer of the Blessed Mary of Overey of the Rectory of Banstead, called Canon Parsonage, had unjustly entered the common called le Hethir Heath by Wykins Cross, with his sheep, where the said Prior hath no common nor ought to common there, and Moys was still offending in 1523 and 1525. After that some sort of settlement was presumably arrived at, but in 1540 the trouble broke out again, for at the Court of 20 October 1540 it was presented that Richard Moyse unjustly occupied the common called Banstead Heath with 200 sheep, and later three of the tenants, Jeffrey Lambert, Roger Lambert, and Thomas Cacott impounded his sheep, with the result that litigation followed.[1] The rolls contain no precise statement of the limits of the right of common, and both parties may have honestly believed in their own claims. At the Court of 5 April 1559 it was ordered on the examination of divers witnesses that the lord and farmer of South Tadworth may have common of pasture in Banstede Hethe for 200 sheep yearly for ever, as they have had of old time by custom.

[1] See i. 167. Moys was a man of substance. 'On the evening of 15 Nov. 1552, between 8 and 9 p.m., George Maneringe late of London, gentleman, Thomas Smarte late of Southwark, yoman, and ten other malefactors broke into his dwelling-house (i.e. Canons) assaulted him and stole a goblett of silver worth 40*s*., a "rattyscolor" cloke worth 40*s*., 60*s*. in money, a "sylver salte" worth 50*s*., four silver spoons worth 10*s*. and three pair of sheets worth £4.' (C. P. R. 7 Edw. VI.)

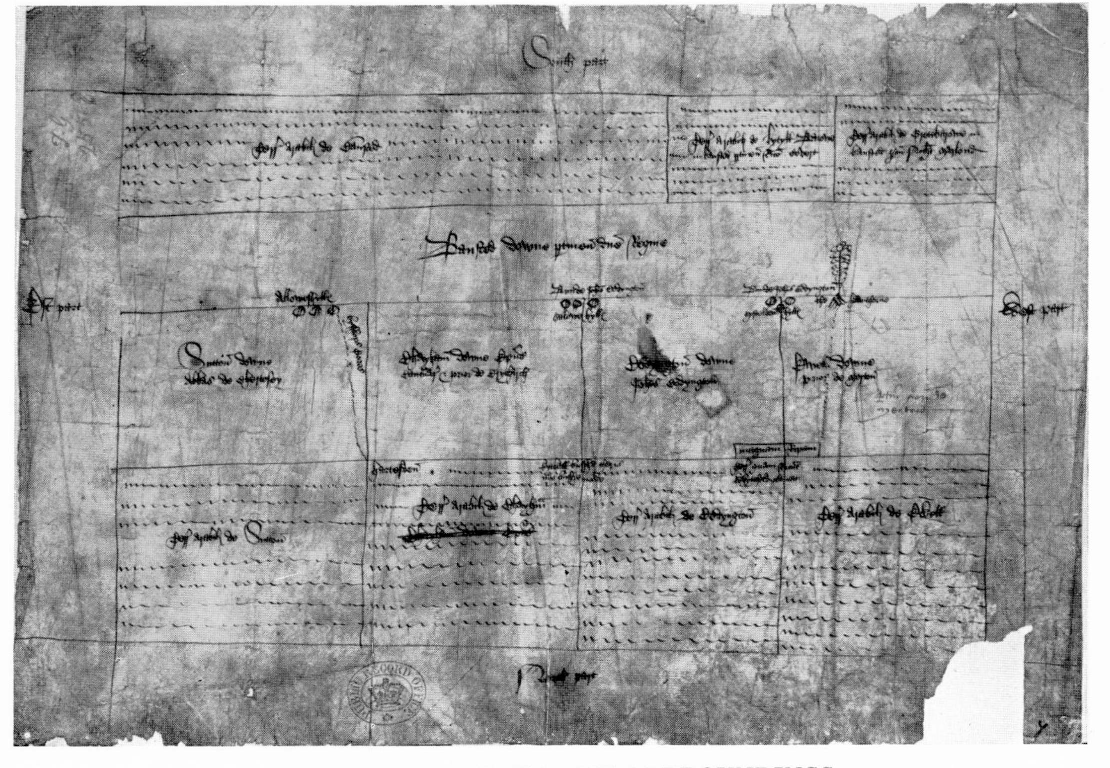

BANSTED DOWNE AND ITS SURROUNDINGS

(*between* 1503 *and* 1536)

But some of the proceedings of other tenants were clearly indefensible. Thomas Staunton, one of the tenants, surcharged the common on the Down with his own sheep and with strange sheep being in his custody contrary to the custom of the manor, and was fined 8*d.* (21 Dec. 1507). William Colcok had no shepherd with his sheep, so that they jumped over hedges and stiles into the lands of divers tenants (19 April 1526). George Kynge of Tadworth persistently surcharged the common, though limited to 200 sheep on Banstead Heath (2 April 1565 and 21 May 1573). At the Court of 23 April 1523 William Richbell of Tadworth the younger was fined 3*s.* 4*d.* for chasing with dogs the sheep of Maud Scoryer and other tenants. And both tenants and strangers are presented at various times for cutting furze or timber, or digging loam, though it was recognized that the tenants of the manor were entitled to dig loam for mending the walls of their tenements (22 Oct. 1527). And encroachments by ploughing, such as that of Thomas Staunton in the common field called Coffadown, were also repressed (21 Oct. 1533; see p. 105).

The picture which the rolls suggest is that of a community whose rights and obligations depended on custom, for the most part entirely unrecorded,[1] faced with economic circumstances which offered strong inducements to disregard that custom. The statement quoted above with regard to the right of common of South Tadworth bases itself on the ancient practice, but it is obvious that it can only have been made because that practice was either unknown or questioned. The Court made some attempts to regulate the right of pasture. On 23 May 1538 it was ordered that no tenant or inhabitant within the lordship having any lands to farm, or of his own, should pasture any sheep in the Common field or on the Common called the Down of Bansted beyond two sheep for each acre which he so held, with a penalty of 4*d.* for each sheep in excess. In 1561 the question of a rate for sheep in Bansted Heth was raised, and at the Court of 5 April 1581 it was ordered that no one was to keep any greater number of sheep in Banstead or Tadworth than for every acre of ground which they shall have by estimation

[1] The elaborate Extent of 1325 (i. 61) is almost entirely concerned with corn farming, and contains very few references to pasture.

but two sheep, and a penalty was attached.[1] No tenant was allowed to pasture his sheep beyond a certain way in the common field called Croydon way before 1 November under a penalty of 3*s.* 4*d.* (21 October 1533), and the Court ordered on 19 September 1570 that no sheep were to be placed in the common field called the Ershe (i.e. stubble) of the manor for three weeks after the first Sunday next following the time that all the corn had been carried away. Pigs were also kept off the Ershe till the first Sunday after the corn was carried, and all other cattle were forbidden. The Court of 11 December 1506 regulated the pasturage in the Frith, i.e. the Freedown or Hundred acres, where the tenants only had access during part of the year,[2] viz. between harvest and 1 November, for 3 acres with 1 horse or for 2 acres with 1 ox or cow, and from 1 November till sowing for each acre with 5 sheep.

Pigs, which did damage by turning up the surface of the commons, were required to be ringed under a penalty of 2*d.* for each animal (21 Oct. 1533),[3] and ducks and geese were forbidden (18 Oct. 1569).

Arable farming received less attention, but on 2 April 1504 the Court ordered that whereas divers tenants having lands in divers shots, of which one is called Bulters Shott, another Holden Shott, and a third abuts on Cheam way, have been used to sow in one shot each year leaving the others unsowed, and some tenants have broken the custom, all tenants in these shots shall sow in the same shots at the same time according to custom, and not otherwise, under a penalty of 40*d.*

The Court also had an eye on some of the grosser infringements of sanitary conditions. On 12 December 1537 the homage presented that whereas the tenants and inhabitants had been accustomed to have the water in the common pond called the Meere, by the house of John Puplett, for brewing, kneading their bread and cooking their food, and the said pond was wont to be kept clean and pure, Puplett permitted his ducks and geese frequently to disturb the pond and make the

[1] The roll is defaced. At a Court of 23 April 1610 it was ordered that no inhabitant shall keep more sheep than two for each acre of land under a penalty at the rate of 12*d.* for each score in excess. This looks as if the previous order had been forgotten.

[2] See i. 63.

[3] p. 105.

water dirty, and he was ordered to keep his ducks and geese out of it under a penalty of 12*d.* It is an unpleasant picture, especially as it is clear from an entry on 23 May next year that Puplett was by no means the only offender. At a View on 24 October 1588 it was ordered that every one who had laid any straw, litter, or dung in any of the highways or streets should remove it before 25 March under a penalty of 6*s.* 8*d.*, and no one was to lay any more in future. Next year an order was made that none should suffer their geese or ducks to come upon any of the Common waters in the parish under the heavy penalty of 12*d.* for each duck or goose (23 October 1589). There is no water in Banstead except surface water and a few deep wells, and the order in the light of John Puplett's case looks like a desperate attempt to protect the drinking supply.

VII

TENANTS OF THE MANOR IN 1653

THE list which follows is taken from one recorded at the Court Baron of the Manor holden on Monday the 9th January A.D. 1653 by Edward Thurland, Esq., steward there, and its purpose was to present that those whose names were marked (i.e. 31 out of the 49) owed suit at this court and had made default, for which every one was amerced 4*d*. Some notes have been added, which in the case of the first half-dozen names supply some personal details, but the purpose of which is generally to give some indication of the connexion of the family with the place similar to that attempted in vol. i. for the fourteenth century.[1] The list is not of course a list, as the Extent of 1325 may have been, of the heads of families resident in the parish. Robert Wilson, who owned South Tadworth, may not have been regarded as a tenant of the manor and does not appear, and on the other hand the list includes tenants in the Weald, many of the names,—Bray, Burstow, Cowper, Killick, Lechford, Turner, Woodman,—being common in the list of contemporary Horley Churchwardens.[2] The Parish Register (referred to as P. R.) should, however, indicate roughly who were in fact resident in Banstead.

The fact that part of the manor lay below the hill must have encouraged intercourse, and a number of families, such as the Killicks and Woodmans, lived in both parts. In the Extent of 1325 Richard Kyriel serves as a standard for services at Banstead. But neither in the survey of 1598 nor in this list of tenants does any Kyriel appear. The list of Horley Churchwardens just referred to shows several Kerrells, and it might be supposed that the name had disappeared from Banstead. But this was not so. Thomas was married, as the Parish Register shows, in 1565, John died in 1601, William in 1632, and Robert Kerrell of Banstead, labourer, whose wife was buried at Banstead in 1685, was himself presented at a Court of 7 April 1656 for grubbing up young ashes.

The name among the tenants showing the oldest connexion

[1] i. 57.

[2] S. A. C. viii. 253.

with Banstead itself is Puplett, which goes back to the Extent of 1325. None of the gentry shows anything at all equal to this, the Lamberts, whose connexion was much older than that of the Buckles or others, only going back to the beginning of the sixteenth century. Bristowe (if it is the same as Burstowe), White (if it is the same family), and Woodman must be the next oldest, then Mathewe and Killick, which latter appears a little before that of Lambert. Many of the familiar medieval names are gone from the list of tenants,—Colcok, Frank, Hill, King, Lomput, atte Mere, Pottesflode, Richbell, Tegge. But it must not of course be supposed that all these names were extinct. Though Colcok, Lomput, atte Mere, and Pottesflode do not appear in the Register, and Tegge fails to reach 1600, Frank and King persist beyond 1653, and Richbell is very common right into the eighteenth century. The members of these latter families in 1653 presumably belonged to the landless labouring class, like the Kerrells.

Sir Christopher Buckle, Kt.	Son of the Sir Christopher who bought Great Burgh, and grandson of Sir Cuthbert Buckle, Lord Mayor of London in 1593. He was b. 1629, d. 1712, m. Elizabeth daughter of Sir William Lewis of Borden, Hants. The name does not appear before 1600.
Edward Lambert, Gent.	Great grandson of John Lambert, who bought Perrotts in 1516 (see i. 159). He inherited the copyhold land (Well Farm) as younger son, and bought Perrotts in 1634 from his elder brother John. He held a small Court appointment (see i. 189). Born 1582, d. 1666, m. Elizabeth daughter of Edward Greene, citizen and goldsmith of London. The name does not appear before 1500.

Richard Harris, Gent.	A D[r]. in Physicke, he married Elizabeth d. of Edward Bysshe of Smallfield, Surrey, and died in 1675.[1] Not before 1600 in P. R.
John Willmott, Gent.	Second son of Simon Wilmot who owned Banstead Place. He was probably a merchant in the Spanish trade (see p. 64 for the Wilmots). The name does not appear before 1600.
John George Trapps, Gent.	Born 1622, d. 1655, son of Andrew Trapps. The name appears in the Parish Register between 1547 and 1667.
Sir John Southcott, K[t].	Of Chaldon. See p. 10. He lived at Albery in Merstham and died in 1685 (M. B. ii. 260).
Margaret Copley, Widdow	This name does not appear in the Parish Register.
Charles Burton, Esq.	Probably the brother of Sir Henry Burton of Carshalton (M. B. ii. 509).
John Leere, Gent.	Name not in P. R.
Samuel Hawkings	Name common in P. R.
Robert Hawkings	
Robert Killick	Killick is common in the P. R. and in the Court Roll back to 1500. It is also common in the Weald.
Ralph Borer	Borer is common in P. R. in the seventeenth century, but not before.
Richard Bowman	As Borer.
John Rogers	The only entry in P. R. before 1653 is the marriage of Robert Rogers with Elizabeth Knapp of Ewell 1642.

[1] See Visitation of Surrey 1662 (Harleian Society). Also below p. 65.

Ralph Killick	
Samuel Lambert Avery Lambert	For the relationship of these other Lamberts to Edward Lambert see pedigree in S. A. C. xvi.
Thomas Puplett John Puplett	Puplet is not only very common in the P. R. and Court Rolls but occurs in the Extent of 1325 and on the Tadworth roll during the gap in the Banstead Rolls.
Andrew Lambert	
John Harber	Not in P. R.
Jaspar Ockley	Not a Banstead family, but see note S. A. C. xvi. 17.
George Gurnett	In P. R., but not before 1600.
Amey Steevens, Widdow	Stevens in various spellings is very common in the P. R. in the seventeenth century and rare in sixteenth. (Under Beryings 1548 the name Vulvyn (p. 22 of Parish Register Society reprint) should apparently be Steven).
Puplett, Widdow John Smyth Avery Puplett	
Robert Cooper	Cooper appears first in P. R. in seventeenth century. Common in the Weald.
Walter Bristowe Bristowe, Widdow	Burstow is common in the medieval Court Rolls in connexion with the Weald (see i. 143). The P. R. only shows Thomas Burstowe married 1593 and Alice Bristow buried 1548.
Thomas Cuddington	Few entries in P. R. None before 1600.
John Lashford	Nothing in P. R. before 1692. The name under various spell-

	ings is common in the Weald. (See i. 158.)
Richard Killick	
Thomas Turner	A few Turner entries in P. R. None before 1600. Common in the Weald.
Thomas Woodman	Woodman is very common in P. R., and appears on the medieval Court Roll (i. 144). The Woodmans are to be found both at Banstead and in the Weald.
Robert Turner	
John Osborne	Some entries in P. R. from 1564 onwards.
Martin Braye	Bray was not a Banstead family, unless the marriage of Thomas Kempsall and Jane Bray 1589 indicates residence. Martin Bray held Wyats and was in 1653 Churchwarden in Horley. (S. A. C. viii. 253.)
John Cuddington	
Richard Mathew	Mathew is very common in P. R. and Court Rolls after they resume. Tadworth Court Roll 1462 gives John Mathewe.
Thomas Mathew	
William Rowley	Not in P. R.
Hugh Mathew	
Edward Turner	
Joanna Lee, Widdow	A number of entries in P. R. in sixteenth and seventeenth centuries.
William White	White is common in P. R. The name appears also on the medieval Court Rolls (i. 143).
Robert Bristowe	

VIII

BANSTEAD IN THE MIDDLE OF THE EIGHTEENTH CENTURY

It is sometimes thought that the eighteenth century is less interesting than earlier centuries, and that though it has long receded beyond the reach of living memory it is still too near us to be worthy of as much attention. But apart from the great value and interest of much of the eighteenth-century work which has come down to us, it is certain that to most of us a sympathetic understanding of the past is easier as we get nearer to our own day, and it may be claimed for the eighteenth century that it is already far enough removed from us to have acquired something of the glamour of the past; while its men and women, its language and social habits, its opinions and its style of building, though they differ from those of our own day, are sufficiently familiar to make us feel that, if by some magic we were to be transported back into it, we should find a world in some respects inferior and in others superior to our own, but one to which we could adapt ourselves without any great difficulty.

Banstead would indeed be different from the Banstead of to-day, but many of the houses which were standing there in 1750 can still be seen, and the personal appearance of some and the handwriting of many of the inhabitants are at least familiar to the writer. The methods of agriculture, though antiquated now, were approaching to the modern, and the general appearance of the parish, if we eliminate the modern houses, the railway and the telephone poles, if we imagine the roads not hard but green, was much what it was before the war and before development began to deface the country.[1] We should indeed wonder to see how much the place had gained in appearance by the absence of modern conveniences, and by the fact that such houses as existed were all the handiwork of people who had a sound sense of proportion and a taste

[1] All the main features of a map of Banstead Place Farm in 1756 can be traced without difficulty on the Ordnance Survey map, though fields have been thrown together and there was more arable.

which was not merely eclectic and ministered to by mechanical production on a large scale. If, however, we wanted to travel to London, or even to fetch a doctor, it must be admitted that we should find the delay exasperating.

The following sketch is based mainly on the papers relating to the administration of the estate of John Lambert, who died intestate in 1762, aged 72. His ledger, written in a fine, clear, bold hand, and showing all his transactions between 1750 and his death, complete inventories of his furniture and effects, and all the bills paid by the administrator, are in my possession. He lived with his sister at Well Farm, a house whose eighteenth-century façade conceals a much older building. He farmed a good deal of land and had no doubt been a farmer all his life, for as youngest son he had succeeded in 1721 to his father's copyhold lands.[1] His father had no doubt also been a farmer. His eldest brother Thomas had lived at Perrotts; another brother, Sir Daniel, an ex-Lord Mayor of London, lived till his death in 1750 at Well House; and his widow lived on there. A nephew, Daniel Lambert (the administrator of the estate), after 1756 lived at Rooksnest, now Rosehill School, and before 1756 Simon Wilmot, a relation by marriage, had lived there. His brother, Edward Lambert, was a good deal at Banstead, so there was a large family circle.

And here it may be permissible to digress for a moment to follow back the earlier inhabitants of Well House, as their names will exemplify how much greater was the part played in the life of the place by family relationship than in our own time. Lady Lambert, who with her husband had bought the house from the representatives of the original Killick owners, before her marriage was Mary Wilmot, and she and her husband came to live there after the death of her uncle, Simon Wilmot, in 1739. He, who had held the house on lease since 1719, is described in a deed of 1727 as 'of Port St. Mary's in Spain, Merchant'. That deed related to a legacy to Mary Edwards, the wife of the Vicar, and her mother had been a Wilmot. Up to 1719, when he died, Edward Griffith had had a lease, and his wife was a Wilmot. The owners at the time of the 1680 survey were Avice Killick and Alexander Lambert (of Wood

[1] See i. 204.

(*a*) Half timber Wing and Chimney in rear

(*b*) Medieval Fireplace

WELL FARM (1919)

Place, Coulsdon) and Jeffrey Lambert (of Woodmansterne) in right of their wives, the sisters of Avice. But the two husbands were cousins, though distant, of Sir Daniel, for they all had a common ancestor in John Lambert, who died in 1533.

In addition to his own land, mostly near Well Farm, John leased from Sir Nicholas Carew the Free Down—that is the Hundred Acres where the Lunatic Asylum was afterwards built—and also certain other land belonging to Mr. Isaac Hughes. 'Mr. Isaac Hughs and Mrs. Sarah Buckle', his second wife (Miss Buckle, as we should say), the daughter of Christopher Buckle, of Great Burgh, who built Nork, were married, according to the Parish Register, in 1747. Hughes lived at Garratts, which was then a fine modern house (built on older foundations), and which, though largely added to, has been little altered, and he also owned Yewlands (which he no doubt acquired through his first wife, Elizabeth Harris). Yewlands was built about 1730, and is clearly distinguishable from the modern additions at each end of it. It closely resembled Rooksnest opposite to it.

And here it may be remarked that at this time very few houses had names, though in some cases they may have been called after the land on which they were built. The name Well Farm never occurs either in John's ledger or in the valuation made after his death or in the executors' accounts. Names such as Rooksnest or Well House seem all to be later, e.g. in the inventory of furniture at Rooksnest in 1765 the house is called simply Mr. Daniel Lambert's late dwelling-house, and Well House in the same year is described, not by its name, but as a customary brick messuage, &c., situate near the well, and is identified by the names of its past and present occupants.

The crops grown, according to the valuation when the farm was let after John's death, were wheat (46 acres), barley (44½ acres), oats (47½ acres), and pease (8½ acres), and some tares, besides apples, pears, and walnuts—John's father had been a great planter of walnuts. There was also some clover, 46 acres of fallow, and 474 sheep and lambs, 6 cows and calves, 8 hogs, and 4 pigs on the farm.

But it is rather with persons than farming that these notes are concerned. The highest-paid man on the farm from 1756 was James Brown, 'Shephard', whose wages were £7 10s. a year. Thomas Watts, evidently his predecessor, had the same, but in 1750 there is a note, 'Md gave him to buy pr shoes as p. promise 5*s*.', so Watts did better than Brown. The other rates of wages are lower, e.g. 'Jno. Sanders my servant', gets £6 10*s*. for a year's service to 29th September, 1751, and for the three following years £7. But after that Sanders, like most of the others, is paid by the week—6*s*. a week, except during harvest, when he gets 9*s*. a week. Benjamin Flint, however, got 10*s*. for harvest in 1753. Men paid by the week evidently did not take much holiday, for in 1755 is the note on payment of 24 weeks' wages to Sanders, 'N.B.—2 Xmas Hollydays excep^{td}'.

It would appear that in the absence of savings banks some of the regular hands left their wages with their employer, e.g. John Foster put his mark to a receipt from the administrator for two and three-quarters years' wages at £7 a year.

The eighteenth century had heard nothing of the equality of the sexes, and the women were paid at a much lower rate. Their usual wage was £4 a year, though Elizabeth Martin rose to £5—perhaps she was head dairymaid. Sarah Martin, sad to say, 'went away without warning', but was allowed a month's wages. These were then at the rate of £2 10*s*. No doubt a flighty young thing.

Hester Cain, a predecessor of Elizabeth Martin, drew £5. The last entry relating to her is:

'To cash p^{d} for 29 weeks wages from 16 July to this 7 Feb. 1752 and went away £2. 17. 0.

To d^{o} to buy something towards Housekeeping, 6*s*.'

The Parish Register shows that that very morning Hester was married to Henry Simmonds, who was for 46 years Parish Clerk, so 'something' was a wedding present.

The receipts for wages given to the Administrator show that most of these people could not sign their names, and writing evidently presented great difficulties to many who were above the position of a hired servant. Here is the bill of the thatcher, Thomas Brown:

'Mr Danil Lambrrt his Bill
for thithing the haystack 4. 0.
for thitching one side of the duck
barn at puden Lane 8 square 1. 0. 0.'

Thatch is no doubt a difficult word to spell, but his next effort, an item for thatching 'at the Whiddo Clark' is no more successful. Puden (pudding) Lane was the Woodmansterne Lane, and as it was of course unmetalled it no doubt deserved its name.

Thomas Richardson, the carpenter (who charged 2*s*. a day); William Lancashire, the wheelwright; Nicholas Travis and Thomas Waterer, the woodmen; William Woodman, the sawyer, all sign their names, as does Mary Harrow, the baker who supplied the bread in 1762 after the funeral for distribution to the poor of Banstead. She, however, found 'shilling' as troublesome to spell as Brown found 'thatch',;

'For nine bushels & haf of Bread at Sicks shielns & atepence Bushel £3 . 3 . 4.'

It should be added that the parish accounts show that throughout the eighteenth century churchwardens and overseers who could not write were rare; they were of course the well-to-do men of the parish.

Let us go through the village and see some of the people to whom John Lambert sold his wheat or barley or apples or beasts, and from whom he bought various things. First, there was the butcher, Robert Hawkins, who on 2 February 1754 'left of his shop', and was succeeded by Edward Chapman (the shop was probably at the south-east corner of the High Street). Hawkins, when he bought calves, paid 2*s*. 8*d*. a stone—the price never varied—and 2*s*. 1*d*. for a fat heifer, weight 73 stone; but in 1754 Chapman began to pay 3*s*. for calves. In 1758 the price rises to 3*s*. 4*d*. and falls next year to 2*s*. 8*d*. In February, 1759, he buys a fat cow, weight 77½ stones, at 2*s*. 4*d*., but except for a few sheep and lambs most of the purchases are calves. Hawkins also bought 'sider apples'. No doubt everyone then made cider.

On the other hand, Chapman charged, in 1761, for his mutton, 3½*d*. a pound; for pork, 4*d*; for veal, 4½*d*.; and for beef, 2*s*. a stone (8 lb.).

Chapman was evidently a man of some education. He wrote a very fair hand, and collected tithe and poor rate.

The smith was Jacob Harrow. In 1755 he was shoeing the carthorses at 8*s*. each per annum, but in 1758 he raised his charge to 10*s*. He was at the same time buying 'sider apples', wheat, &c., and the rise in his charge may perhaps be explained by the note: '£1.7.0 not paid to be allowed out of his next Bill, being distressed for money.' Anyhow, poor Jacob died, and his widow, who carried on the business with a man named Gosden, charged 8*s*. again. The long bills for repairs to ploughs, &c., were no doubt written by Gosden, for Elizabeth Harrow put her mark to the receipts.

John Ingram (or Ingrams or Ingrimes) kept the Woolpack,[1] and we naturally find him selling 'granes' to John Lambert, and buying his apples for 'sider' at 1*s*. 2*d*. a bushel and supplying 'Bear for ye apple grinders, 1/-'. For the 4th of March, 1762, the day of John's funeral, he sends in a bill for 'Beer and baco, For pudden, For Bread, butter, etc., For Dreassen'—in all, 13*s*. 4*d*.—a dinner for the bearers; and he duly signs the receipt. But his activities were by no means confined to keeping an inn. He was also a barber, and shaved John, and supplied him with the wigs which eighteenth century respectability demanded. In September, 1756, is an item: 'By a new wig, £3 . 0 . 0. By new making the old one & Hair added, 14 . 0'. But the added hair must have worn off, or the new wig worn out, for in February, 1759, a new wig is charged, £1 15*s*. 0*d*., and two years later yet another one.

The parish did all its business at the Woolpack (except what it did at the Tangier).[2] So under his churchwardens' account John Lambert enters 'pd. at ye Woolpack on settling George Harrison's accounts, 2*s*. 6*d*.', and when as churchwarden he pays for 'Ringing State days' it is to J^{no} Ingram. Ringing the church bells at that time was clearly as impossible without beer as was the conduct of parish business, and Ingrimes must have been a prosperous man.

Samuel Morris was a bricklayer, or rather a small builder, who owned some land of his own. He was employed in doing various repairs to the church,[3] where, if his work was not of a very high order, it was less mischievous than that of successors with more pretensions, and also in building a Parish House (i.e., a Poor House). Unfortunately none of his detailed bills

[1] In 1765 he was paying a rent of £21 for the Woolpack.
[2] See i. 228
[3] i. 233.

remain except the charge for 'taking up a stone and paving in the church for Mr John Lambert and laing off downe. Time and morter and paving Tiles com to £1 . 1 . 0.'—the usual horrid practice of intra-mural burial. Morris must have been a man of some education despite his erratic spelling, for he was also a collector of taxes.

William Steward was the carrier, and after his death his widow continued the business. She charges *2d.* in 1762 for bringing 'a parcil of tea down'. And 'four pounds of solt peter cost 4*s*. For bringing the peter down, *2d.*', and 'a dussin of wine down', 9*d*. As she only put her mark someone else devised the spelling. But the bulk of the carriage of goods from a distance must have been done by the farmers, for there being no water carriage, no one else then possessed any considerable motive power. John Lambert in fact did a good deal of carting. For instance, he carts 'Load Goods from London 15*s*.' for Lady Lambert pretty regularly each spring besides carting coals ('carriage 2 chaldron coales from London £1'), and mould and dung, probably for the Well House garden. Similarly, he carts for Isaac Hughes '3 chaldron coales from Kingston £1 . 1 . 0', to which he adds '4*d*. per chaldron for Beer by Custom', but as he subsequently carted more coals without charging for the beer, Mr. Hughes may be supposed to have resented the customary payment. Again, in 1754, he carried '2 Load Goods to Mitcham for Madam Haltien', the widow of James Haultain, who lived in Banstead, perhaps at Yewlands, and had died the year before. In March, 1761, he carts 2,000 bricks for Saml Morris to Ewell. He also carts oats for his brother Edward, 'delivered att his House in London' (Edward, who lived in Southwark, was a woolstapler, and John sold him wool). Edward, it should be added, reciprocated by getting various things for John—hops, tea, brandy, tobacco, a Gloucester cheese, vinegar, and so forth. It is curious that in 1753 Edward should buy butter for him in London, but the account seems to imply that this was so. All the little things no doubt came down by the carrier, unless Edward brought some of them when he rode down in the summer. From 1752 onward he kept his horse in the winter with his brother at Banstead, paying 1*s*. a week. As he was 72 in 1752 (he lived to be 82), it may be supposed that he found riding down in winter too trying.

The vicars at this time were John Edwards[1] and James Wagstaffe. The former held office from 1714 to 1754, the latter from 1754 to 1789, and if we add to these the tenures of their immediate predecessor and successor, it will be found that from soon after the Restoration till into the reign of George IV Banstead had only four vicars, that is, in 161 years, an average tenure of forty years for each vicar. The vicar, however, will only appear here as the recipient of tithe, which, before the passing of the Tithe Act of 1839, was apt to be a source of trouble; so much so, indeed, that Stevenson in his Agriculture of Surrey (1813) argued that the uncertainty of tithe seriously depreciated the value of a tithed farm, even when let at a reduced rent, as compared with one that was tithe-free. It was usual to pay a composition per acre, and this was in fact done at Banstead in 1762 with the great tithe, which then, as now, belonged to Newport Grammar School. The basis was 4*s.* 6*d.* per acre under wheat; barley, 3*s.*; oats, 2*s.* 6*d.* (In a paper headed 'Tithe of Banstead Place Farme', 3 acres under tares and 15 under clover are included at 2*s.* 6*d.*, and these are presumably included in the total under 'oats, &c.,' debited to 'M^r^. Phineas Cotes, Esq.,' of Banstead Place.)

The vicar's tithe must have been more troublesome. Here it is, for 1762, on John Lambert's land:

		£	*s.*	*d.*
106	Lambs at 3*d.*	1	6	6
6	Calves at 4*d.*		2	0
1	Barren Cow at 2*d.*			2
1,700	Bavins at 1/8		17	0
300	Kiln Bavins at 10*d.*		2	6
2½	hundred Tods at 1/-		2	6
1	hundred Stakes at		3	0
21	Hirdles at 2½*d.*		4	4
	Hoops		5	0

[1] William Romaine (1714–95), later a famous preacher and a supporter of Whitefield, was his curate. He found an opening in London through being made chaplain by Sir Daniel Lambert when Lord Mayor in 1741. See Romaine's Works (1796) vii. 16.

72 lb. of Wool at 6½*d*	1	19	0
a Pig		2	0
Easter offering		5	0

The paper is receipted by Wagstaffe in his beautifully clear Italian hand. Edwards also wrote a good hand—not so good as Wagstaffe's, but better than most hands of to-day.

There are a few dealings in the papers with people outside Banstead: Widow Wells of Cheam, a maltster; George Carter the mason, who charged 2*s.* a dozen for 132 letters on the memorial stone; and some others. One is Mr. Francis Hutchins, from whom in 1757 John Lambert had a yard and a half of superfine cloth at 17*s.* a yard. He was probably either a merchant or a ship's captain who commanded one of the ships engaged in the Oporto or Spanish trade, in which the Wilmots and some of the Lamberts were interested. Simon Wilmot owned a ship named the *Banstead*, and one of John's nephews had been at Oporto for many years. An extract from a letter written home four years after John's death by his great nephew, Thomas Lambert, at Oporto, brings home the difficulties of communication at the time very vividly: 'Poor [Captain] Bradshaw has been out a long time. He says he laid five weeks in Portland Road, two anchors out all the while, and hard gales of wind at South West.' The posts between Oporto and Banstead were erratic, and there was small inducement for ordinary folk to travel far for pleasure.

One other bill must be mentioned, that of Samuel Horne, the apothecary, who attended John in his last illness. Banstead, of course, had no doctor of its own, and Horne made 32 journeys (? from Epsom) between 6 January and 22 February to Banstead, besides two journeys to London—perhaps for consultation or to get special medicine. For this and for numerous 'draughts', 'cordial nervose boluses', and what not, he charged £13 11*s.* 2*d.* But they were of no effect, for the old man died on 24 February, and was buried in Banstead Church on the 4th of March.

The cost of his funeral was over £33, which may seem to us a good deal of money, but it was small compared with other cases. His brother Nicholas, who died at or near Kentish Town in 1755, was brought to Banstead Church to be buried at a cost of over £58, which included a hearse drawn by six horses covered with black velvet trappings, with plumes of black feathers, and there were two porters riding in mourning gowns with staves covered with black silk. The four mourning coaches had six horses each. This, however, was probably not mere display, for the roads were bad. The relatives were all supplied with mourning cloaks, and there were further clothes and trappings for the clergy and clerks and servants, in addition to which over £10 was spent on miscellaneous expenses, such as the clerk's fee and expenses at the Woolpack—no doubt the dinner for the bearers. Besides all this £30 was spent on distributing mourning rings, and £75 on the monument in Banstead Church. These sums were not out of the way, and are in fact less than what was spent on the funeral of his son in 1765. Eighteenth-century funeral monuments are often impressive and sometimes beautiful; that for instance to Sir Daniel Lambert in the South aisle is an admirable piece of stately funeral eulogy. But they were of course the outcome of an attitude towards death, which was somewhat different from our own.

One other point may be worth mentioning. The executors found no less than £59 14*s.* 3*d.* in John Lambert's purse. But this was not unusual. His brother's executors in 1755 found money in a bag, £51 15*s.* 2*d.*, and it was no doubt necessary to keep large sums in the house in the days before a banking system had been developed.

BANSTEAD CHURCH

From Cracklow's Views of Surrey Churches (1823)

IX

NOTES ON PLACES IN THE PARISH

Apsley Cottage

This house preserves the name of Alexander Apsley, who lived for many years at Banstead Place, and died in 1827. He bought the land in 1797 from some of the Morris family (who owned the Mint Farm) and probably built the existing house. The long strip of land on the other side of the road was formerly waste of the manor, and was granted to him in 1805.

Banstead Downs

Much the earliest map in which Banstead appears is the map or diagram preserved in the Record Office, of which a reproduction is given (see p. 54), with a key for those who find the scale unduly reduced. It shows how much downland in the neigh-

<table>
<tr><td></td><td colspan="4">South</td><td></td></tr>
<tr><td rowspan="4">East</td><td colspan="2">Arable land of Bansted</td><td>Arable land of Lytyll Barowe in Bansted belonging to Ric. Covert</td><td>Arable land of Grete Barowe in Bansted belonging to Nic. Marlond</td><td rowspan="4">West</td></tr>
<tr><td colspan="4">Bansted Downe belonging to the Queen</td></tr>
<tr><td>Sutton Downe
Abbot of
Chertesey</td><td>Chayham Downe
Archbishop of Canterbury and Prior of Christchurch</td><td>Codyngton
Downe
John
Codyngton</td><td>Ewell Downe
Prior of
Merton</td></tr>
<tr><td>arable land
of
Sutton</td><td>arable land
of
Chayham</td><td>arable land
of
Codyngton</td><td>arable land
of
Ewell</td></tr>
<tr><td></td><td colspan="4">North</td><td></td></tr>
</table>

bouring parishes has failed to survive the movement for enclosure. The Queen, to whom Banstead Downe belonged, was Queen Catherine, and the date of the map must be between 1503 and 1536.[1]

The John Codyngton referred to was the owner of Cuddington Manor (later merged in Ewell) 'which is adjoyninge to the Downys called Bansted Downys belongynge to the Kings Highnesse'.[2] He seems to have been a bad neighbour. In April 1516, according to the Court Roll, he unjustly occupied Banstead Downe with his sheep, and in October he still had 800 sheep there of his own and his tenant's. And although he had very often been warned, he did not cease to do so. In 1521 he was presented as depasturing 400 sheep on the common of the lady of the manor called Brounhethe, and was fined 40*d.*, and a similar fine was inflicted in 1525 on him for having 600 sheep on Banstead Downe to the prejudice of the lady and her tenants. The map is probably connected with some of the disputes about the right of pasture referred to in Chapter VI.

For Ewell Downe at a later date see under Warren Farm.

Boulters Pond

The pond has now been filled up in the interests of motor traffic and the trees fringing it have been cut down. The pictures show what the appearance of the place used to be.

Although Boulters Lane existed at least as far back as 1557 (i. 275) it was only accepted by the Parish in 1855 as a Parish road. It had then been widened by Mr. Alcock.

Buff House

This house was built about 1800, perhaps by Walter Borrowes, late of Mincing Lane, who in any case seems to have lived there for a short time. In particulars of sale (1 July 1806) it is described as a very valuable cottage residence, furnished in a style of peculiar neatness with handsome solid mahogany doors, bow windows, veranda, &c., and planted with valuable shrubs and evergreens.

[1] R. O. Special Collections, Rentals and Surveys, 15/29 and 20/18. See S. A. C. xxxiv. 20 for a discussion of the reasons for the date assigned.

[2] Augmentation Office Survey quoted by M. B. ii. 599.

In summer (1928)

In winter (*c.* 1910)

BOULTER'S POND

The belt of trees which formerly fringed the road to the west in a pleasing curve which perpetuated the irregularity of a road which went back to Saxon times has been cut down for development, and the road will be straightened in the interests of motor traffic.

The Church

The deed of Nigel de Moubray, granting an orchard and five acres to the Canons of Southwark, is printed in the Appendix. The orchard is clearly the little orchard to the north of the church, and if Mr. Malden is right in dating the grant approximately 1170 (S. A. C. xxxi. 134), which is ten years earlier than the earliest date assigned by Mr. P. M. Johnston to any part of the existing building, this would show that the existing church must be on the site of the earlier church. This is antecedently probable, but the dating is uncertain.

Cracklow's view shows the church as it was in or before 1823. The North Chapel since the war has been made a War Memorial Chapel, and the organ has been placed above the tower-arch without advantage to the music or architecture of the building.

Garratts

No record seems to have survived to fix the date of the existing house, but it appears to be about 1700, though it incorporates older elements. The Elizabethan chimney-piece in the Library, which bears the date 1584 and the initials R.L and E.L., comes from Shortes Place in Woodmansterne, and after that house was pulled down (see S. A. C. xvi. 20 for a picture of the house) the chimney-piece with some of the wainscotting of the parlour of the Elizabethan house was given by Mr. William Lambert in 1868 to Mr. John Lambert, who then lived at Garratts, and was there re-erected. The initials stand for Roger Lambert (buried at Banstead 1617) and Elizabeth Lambert (buried at Banstead 1633).

Mint Farm

The name is modern, for it is that of a crop which has not been long cultivated at Banstead, though it may go back into the eighteenth century. The house is much older, and in one of the bedrooms upstairs there is a stone fireplace with a flat

Tudor Arch. The older name was Farmecroft. In 1697 John Morris of Banstead, bricklayer, bought one moiety and in 1711 the other moiety of a messuage and lands commonly called Farmecroft, and in 1783 it is called Farmcrofts. The name no doubt represents the Farnycroft of the 1325 survey.

Park Downs

The author's house called Larklands (which was built in 1912–13) stands at the top of a bank which runs from the eastern side of the parish along the top of Park Downs to Holly Lane. Although what was in 1801 the arable field called Larklands, and Peacocks field, and the three fields marked Ten acres, Crooked twelve acres, and Chalk pit Hook on the tithe map all lie below the bank, it seems clear that the bank marks the old dividing line between the cultivated land and the common, and has been created by centuries of ploughing, for where the plough stopped on the slope a double process went on, the bushes growing and holding up the soil above, while it washed away below, so that the height of the bank is some measure of its antiquity. (A similar but smaller bank exists at the bottom of Larklands.) Not only are Larklands and Peacocks field obviously enclosures from the common, but there is good reason to suppose that the others are also, for the acreage of la Hoke was 39½ acres in 1325 (39 acres in 1364) whereas in 1540 la Hooke contained 60 acres, and in 1680 seven parcels of arable called Hookes contained 74 acres, which is approximately the same as on the tithe map. Now the acreage of the three fields marked Ten acres, Crooked twelve acres (which in 1801 were called Truman Hooks and Bottom Hooks) and Chalk Pit Hooks is just over 30½ acres, which added to the 39½ acres of 1325 comes near enough to the 74 acres of 1680 on the tithe map. This is so especially if you allow for the road, which in 1680 and even in 1841 must have been the merest track, for in the latter year six ratepayers at a vestry declared that the Parish was not liable to repair the road from Mr. Steer's house (Court farm) to Park Downs. We may take it, therefore, that the acreage of Park Downs was considerably larger in the fourteenth century than it was later.

These reductions of the Common seem to have gone to swell

PART OF A (? SEVENTEENTH CENTURY) MAP SHOWING PRESTON DOWNS AND THE BARROWS

the demesne lands and, in the case of Peacocks field, the lands of another landowner,[1] without any reservation of the tenants' rights such as was made when the Freedown was taken in from Banstead Downs some time before 1325,[2] the reason no doubt being the changed conditions of farming, which was increasingly carried on in enclosed fields. But the process of enclosure reached its limits, and we have been left with over 1300 acres of common in the parish, mainly because, as Stevenson insisted, it was not profitable to break them up. 'Though it is impossible', he says, 'exactly to fix the value of the Downs (in Surrey—he refers especially to Banstead, Epsom, and Clandon) yet a slight inspection of the grass which the best of them yield, will probably convince those who contend that they ought to be broken up, that a certain advantage would thus be destroyed for the sake of a very uncertain profit. Few kinds of soil support such a close, healthy, and nourishing sward as the Downs do: and few kinds of soil pay worse while under the plough, or are so difficult to be converted into grass again, if once broken up.' (General View of the Agriculture of the County of Surrey, 1813.)

The large chalk pit on Park Downs must be of great antiquity. The Court Roll of 20 April 1425 shows that it was found by view of the Steward and other tenants that John Wethemere cut thorns growing on the old pit at le Brokenhyll (i.e. Park Downs, see i. 292) and made there a hedge without licence.

At a Court of 10 December 1801 it was presented that the chalk pit was dangerous.

Preston

The site of the Chapel, which is marked on the Ordnance map, is easily recognizable, but only foundations remain. The building measured approximately 30 feet from East to West and 15 feet from North to South (inside measurements). Edwards records many human bones being found in Preston wood.[3]

The old map, part of which is here reproduced, is referred to by Manning and Bray as 'an ancient and very rudely drawn

[1] The field called Peacocks field on the tithe map (a name which it evidently got from its owner) was called Bottom Close or Limekiln field in 1680 (i. 214).

[2] i. 63.

[3] i. 249. See also St. Leonards, Preston, in S. A. C. xxxvii.

plan of part of Mr. Buckle's Estate'.[1] It shows Preston Downs, on which is written 'The distresse taken'. It was, therefore, probably compiled for use in litigation, but the occasion is unknown. As, however, it shows the three lordships of Preston, Burgh, and North Tadworth, it is presumably earlier than 1663, when Christopher Buckle added North Tadworth to Burgh and Preston, which his father had purchased in 1614. It is no doubt that map which Sir Christopher,[2] when he was disputing with Sir Richard Buckley and other inhabitants of Ewell about the boundaries of the parish, took out of his pocket, showing it to Buckley and pointing out the boundaries. But Buckley was not impressed, and asked whether he had nothing better on which to base his title, himself producing a survey of the time of Elizabeth.[3] The map was not apparently produced at either of the actions about the Ewell boundaries in the time of George II (see under Warren Farm). It is now in my possession.

The map is particularly interesting on account of the barrows, all of which have now disappeared (see further as to this under Warren farm). Some further remarks on this map and such other maps of Banstead before the tithe map as are known to me to exist will be found in S. A. C. xxxiv.

Rooksnest, or Rosehill School

The old part of this building, which is the block containing the five windows to the right as you face the present front door, dates from the same time as Yewlands, which it closely resembles, i.e. *c.* 1730. Like Yewlands, it had originally a front door in the middle of the block, which was replaced by a window when the present front door was made, and like Yewlands, a row of old lime trees, evidently coeval with the house, stand in front of it.

Town Field

This is described on the tithe map as Town Field or Pound Field, but the latter appears to be merely a corruption. The

[1] i. 254. M. B.'s diagram of part of the map is not very accurate.

[2] His father died in 1660, but he was only knighted in 1681. He died in 1712, and Sir Richard Buckley in 1710.

[3] From the deposition of Thomas Bartlett, one of the witnesses for the plaintiff in *Lewen* v. *Buckle* (1740) in R.O. (E 133/83/7).

remaining part of it was presented in 1925 by Miss Neville to the Parish Council to carry out the wish of her late brother and in memory of her mother, Lady Neville, widow of Sir Ralph Neville, who for many years lived at Banstead Place. It was renamed the Lady Neville Recreation Ground.

Tumble Beacon

The Tumble Beacon has been scheduled under an order in Council of 9 October 1924, under the Ancient Monuments Consolidation and Amendment Act 1913. But it has been damaged by being included in the garden of a house which has been built close up to it. For what it was, see the picture in i. 253.

Wardons

This was identified (i. 302) with Well Farm, not quite correctly. The customary messuage or tenement and 100 acres called Warders alias Wardons, and 5 acres of wood to which William Lambert (of Woodmansterne) was admitted in 1771 on the death of his father John, included a number of fields (Stoneylands, Old Burry, &c.) which were subsequently included in Well Farm, but Wardons itself, which was at the corner by the Well, stood in what is now part of Yewlands. In 1848 it was occupied by William Reigate, and when the (Woodmansterne) Lambert property in Banstead was sold in that year the house and 7 acres of Hollands meadow were bought by the Rev. Peter Aubertin of Chipstead. In the sixteenth century the property belonged to the Killick family. Richard Killick surrenders a tenement called Warders to the use of Thomas Killick and his heirs in 1553, and in 1617 the death of Robert Killick who held a tenement and 100 acres called Warders is presented.

Warren Farm

Before 1731 this was a rabbit warren and sheep-walk. In 1647 Sir Christopher Buckle, of Borough in Bansted, let to William White, of Cannhatch in Bansted, all that his warren of conyes situated in Greate Borough commonly called Greate Borough warren with a lodge or warren house upon the said warren (not the existing house) with liberty to keep and kill conyes there and upon Greate Borough Sheepe Downe or Sheepewalk adjoining.[1]

About 1731 the then owner Christopher Buckle began to plough up some of the grass land, and enclosed and converted it into a farm, letting most of it to a tenant named John Smith. His neighbour, however, George Lewen, of Ewell (whose daughter and sole heir married Sir Richard Glyn) claimed that Buckle had ploughed up part of Ewell Downs, and that as holding the Rectory of Ewell he was himself entitled to the tithes. His servants removed some of Smith's corn, who thereupon, supported by Buckle, brought an action for trespass in the Court of Common Pleas, which was tried at Kingston in 1735, and a special jury after viewing the land gave a verdict for Smith. Legal proceedings against Buckle were begun in the Exchequer in 1738 by Lewen, who claimed that 40 acres of the land ploughed up were in Ewell, as was shown by a survey of the Parish and Manor of Ewell made in 1577 by one Taylor, County Surveyor.[2] Buckle produced evidence to show that he and his ancestors had exercised the rights of ownership, that the small tithes had been paid to the Vicar of Banstead, and that the perambulations of the parish had always included the land in dispute in Banstead. The dispute was evidently of old standing (see p. 78), and both sides produced the evidence of the oldest inhabitants, who testified with equal confidence to the bounds which their respective perambulations had followed. No decree appears to be recorded, so the action was probably dropped.

The depositions, apart from the question where exactly the boundary of the parish ran, contain some interesting points. The name of the sheep-walk was Rosebushes hill or Preston hill and East Down hill. Continual reference is made to what were probably barrows, such as 'the three knowls or little hills where the parishes of Ewell, Cuddington, and Bansted meet in a

[1] This deed, which was one of those produced in the eighteenth century litigation, is in my possession. For the legal proceedings referred to see Exchequer Bills and Answers (E. 112), Geo. II, Surrey, No. 261, and the depositions for Buckle taken by Commission, 14 Geo. II, Trinity, No. 2, Surrey in R. O. The depositions for Lewen are in E. 133/83/7.

[2] Evidently that referred to at p. xxii of the Register or Memorial of Ewell (1913). The survey in 1740 had been in the possession of the Earl of Scarborough and was then in the custody of his executor.

(*a*) Left-hand spandrel of Fireplace

(*b*) Right-hand spandrel of Fireplace

WELL FARM (1919)

point'. These tended no doubt to disappear with ploughing (as indeed we know that barrows disappeared[1]), and one witness speaks of 'a place called by this deponent the Long Hill, where there are now two knowles, and where there was formerly three knowles'.

Some evidence regarding horse-racing was given by John Watson of Carshalton, gentleman, aged 67 or thereabouts. His late brother, Devereux Watson, was, he said, about 54 years before 'Clerk of the races upon Bansted Downes called Bansted Downes Course', and, as he told deponent, paid an acknowledgement of 5*s*. a year to Rouse, who was then Buckle's tenant, for leave for horses running over the north part of a piece of land called the Great Borough Warren and a piece of land called Sir Christopher Buckle's sheep-walk in Bansted. This was continued for about thirty years. The course was carried over the said warren about 30 rod, leaving the Warren house on the right and about 4 or 5 rod, on the left hand of Beach Cross,[2] where there is now a pond, and so over Mr. Buckle's sheep-walk now converted into tillage.

Well Farm

Although the front of the house is only early eighteenth century this (as was often done) was put on to a much older timber framed building, the centre part of which is late fifteenth century. The south-west end is Elizabethan. In a first floor room at the back the fire-place shown in the picture had long been known to exist, and since the war a similar fire-place was discovered in the room below by the then owner, Sir Guy Standing. The fire-place on the first floor with the sacred monogram in the spandrels can, in the opinion of Mr. P. M. Johnston, hardly be later than about 1480,[3] and the question naturally arises who built the house. The Court Roll shows that Richard at Wode on 6 November 1493 sold all his

[1] See i. 255 and p. 78 of this volume.

[2] There are many references to Beech Cross and other crosses. William Clark of Banstead, one of Lewen's witnesses, deposed that by Buckle's orders, he had, with a shepherd employed by Smith, Buckle's tenant, taken stones out of a cross laid down by the Ewell people, and put turf down.

[3] In his article in S. A. C. xxxiii, Well [House] Farm, Banstead.

copyhold lands to Thomas Wynnam, citizen and baker of London. At Wode is a name which appears in the Extent of 1325, and Richard was probably the man who in 1488 brewed and sold mede without a licence and was then made constable.[1] He is an unlikely builder. Wynnam was evidently a speculator, for in April 1495 he sold to Master Robert Sherborne, who was a fellow of New College, Oxford, employed by Henry VII on various missions, and in 1499 was made Dean of St. Paul's. He was frequently abroad, and was fined for non-attendance at the manorial court. In May 1505 the Court Roll shows that Sherborne 'modo menevensis episcopus' sold to William and George Warham, sons of Nicholas Warham. Now Sherborne by forging a Papal bull, had just succeeded in becoming Bishop of St. Davids[2] (Menevia, 12 April 1505) and was Bishop of Chichester from 1508 till his death in 1536. George Warham sold his half share to William Muschamp, and in 1516 Muschamp and William Warham sold to John Lambard, in whose family the Well Farm remained till 1919. The most likely builder among these various owners was Sherborne—the sacred monogram is suitable to him, and he is nearer to Mr. Johnston's date (1480) than either the Warhams or John Lambert. The latter, it might be added, seems to have been living at Well Farm at the time of his death in 1533, and his descendants also to have lived there (and not at Perrotts as is suggested in i. 250) until the eighteenth century (see Well House), the last who lived there being that John Lambert (d. 1762) whose papers furnished the substance of much of Chapter VIII.

Well House

The date at which the older part of Well House was built is not known, but it appears to be about the middle of the seventeenth century. In 1680 it belonged to members of the Killick family.[3] Sir Daniel Lambert, who bought the house, lived there from 1739 to his death in 1750, and as he built the dining-room wing this can be dated between those years. In 1746 he acquired a strip of land to the west of the garden, on

[1] i. 156.
[2] See Letters of Henry VII, i. 246 (Rolls Series).
[3] i. 204. See also p. 64 of this volume.

which he built a brick wall. The exact point at which it joined up to the older wall can easily be detected.

In 1821 the house was advertised as to let, and was described (Times, 6 September) as a desirable residence for a family of respectability, consisting of an excellent dining-room, drawing-room, &c., and it was added that three packs of hounds were kept in the neighbourhood.

The appearance of the house was somewhat damaged when, in or about 1832, in order to get more accommodation one of the seventeenth-century gables was replaced by a slate roof.

APPENDIX OF DOCUMENTS

I

GRANT (UNDATED) BY NIGEL DE MOWBRAY OF AN ORCHARD AND FIVE ACRES TO THE CONVENT OF SOUTHWARK [1]

Nigellus de Moubrai omnibus hominibus suis francis et anglis et universis Sancte Matris ecclesie filiis tam presentibus quam futuris; salutem. Notum sit omnibus vobis me concessisse et dedisse et hac mea carta confirmasse deo et beate Marie et Canonicis ecclesie sancte Marie de Sudwurch' in liberam et perpetuam elemosinam pomerium quod est apud aquilonem inter ecclesiam de Benested et viam que graditur apud domum Vitalis de Sutt' et inter viam que ducit ad curiam meam et semitam que in occidente ducit ad Ecclesiam. Et v acras in Hamma. habendum et possidendum sicut liberam et perpetuam et quietam elemosinam ex omni seculari servitio et exactione tenendum de me et heredibus meis eternaliter. Hanc vero elemosinam optuli super altare Sancte Marie in Ecclesia de Sudwerch' pro salute mea et uxoris mee et omnium propinquorum meorum. His testibus. Ricardo de Hasting'. Willelmo Capellano. Rogero de Moubrai. Ricardo de Alvers. Roberto de Buci. Roberto filio Rogeri. Vitali de Sutt'. Willelmo de Coveh'. Gocelino Vinatore. Radulpho Vinatore. Radulpho Bucell'. Waltero de Well'. Michaele filio Radulphi de Cornh'. Petro preposito et aliis quam pluribus.

II

I.P.M. OF MARGARET, COUNTESS OF KENT (1258) I.P.M., HENRY III, 23/16 (C. 132)

Inquisicio facta apud Benstede die Sabbati in vigilia Sancti Andree anno rengni[2] regis Henrici filii Johannis regis xliij scilicet de terris et tenementis que fuerunt Margarete quondam Comitissa[2] Kancie die quo obiit in Surreia et de quo tenentur Dicunt juratores scilicet Galfridus de la Wodecot Fabr' benor [et ?] broke Alanus le King Fabr' de Feringcroft Lucas de Aula Rogerus filius Luce Galfridus de Suttone Willelmus le Kure Fabr' de la Le Johannes

[1] See S. A. C. xxxi. 134 with photographic facsimile. For the five acres see i. 378. Canonhams on the tithe map is 4A. 2R. 21P.

[2] So in MS.

de Apeldrele Johannes de . . . Johannes de Poneshurst Willelmus Atenore Willelmus de Apeldrele Willelmus de Ponte Isti dicunt quod predicta Margareta tenuit manerium de Benstede de Rogero de Munbrey pro tribus feodis militum et idem Rogerus tenet de rege in capite et dicunt quod de manerio habentur de redditu assise v marce et habentur due carucate terre dicti manerii valor c s. et valent pastura bosci etc per annum ij marce et dimidia et valet gardinum dimidia marca Et dicunt quod Johannes de Burk propincquior heres ejus est Et est etatis.

III

INQUISITION AS TO FAILURES OF RENT AT BANSTEAD (1354)

(Spec. Coll. Ministers Accounts, 1010/11)

Inquisicio capta de decasibus reddituum et serviciorum in manerio de Banstede ad Curiam tentam ibidem die lune in festo Apostolorum Simonis et Jude anno xxviij° per sacramentum totius homagii qui dicunt

. . . redd' et servic' terre vocate Solelond per annum x*s*.

[Furselonde] . . . terre et ferthinglonde de redditu et serviciis per annum ij*s*. ix*d*. ob. q.

Item de tenemento quondam Dusebard de redditu et serviciis per annum v*s*. iij*d*.

Item [de tenemento] quondam Willelmi atte Strete de redditu et serviciis per annum iiij*s*. xj*d*. et iij vomeribus precii iij*s*.

Item de [tenemento quondam] . . . Thes (?) de redditu et serviciis per annum v*s*. v*d*. et ij vomeribus precii ij*s*.

Item de [tenemento quondam Nicholai] Monek de redditu et serviciis per annum iiij*s*. xj*d*. et j vomere precii xij*d*.

Item de terra quondam . . . de redditu et serviciis per annum vj*s*. vij*d*. ob. et j vomere precii xij*d*.

Item de tenemento quondam Symonis Bode de redditu et serviciis per annum ij*s*. x*d*. ob.

Item de tenemento de Boytone de redditu et serviciis per annum xx*d*. ob. q.

Item [de tenemento] quondam Johannis Longe de redditu et serviciis per annum v*s*. ix*d*. et j vomere precii xij*d*.

Item de tenemento quondam Thome Cole de redditu et serviciis per annum vij*s*. j*d*.

Item de tenemento quondam Petri atte Hacche de redditu et serviciis per annum ij*s*.

Item de tenemento quondam Roberti atte Hacche de redditu et serviciis per annum xix*d*. q.

Item de tenemento quondam Galfridi Cole de redditu et serviciis per annum x*s*. iiij*d*. et dimidio vomere precii vj*d*.

Item de tenemento quondam Willelmi Dongehulle de redditu et serviciis per annum v*s*. xj*d*. et j gallina precii ij*d*. ob.

Item de j curtilagio et vij acris terre quondam Johannis filii Vicarii de redditu et serviciis per annum vij*s*. ij*d*.

Item de vij acris terre quondam Simonis in the Lane per annum vj*s*.

Item de terra vocata Vydelond et j Joinereselond per annum vj*s*. vij*d*.

Item de tenemento quondam Thome Bures de redditu et serviciis per annum iij*s*. vj*d*.

Item de j acra terre quondam Ade Cole per annum v*d*.

Item de j acra terre quondam Elye in the Lane per annum iiij*d*.

Item de tenemento quondam Willelmi atte Hide de redditu et serviciis per annum ij*s*. vj*d*. ob. q.

Item de tenemento quondam Walteri [Hugon] de redditu et serviciis per annum vj*s*. j*d*. ob. q. et ij gallinis precii v*d*.

Item de tenemento quondam Henrici Turnor de redditu et serviciis per annum viij*s*.

Item de j acra terre quondam Alicie Potteflode de redditu et serviciis per annum iij*d*.

Item de tenemento quondam Willelmi Hugon de redditu et serviciis per annum iij*s*. vj*d*. q.

Item de tenemento Godardi Thurston de redditu et serviciis per annum vj*s*. ob.

Summa decasuum reddituum cum vomeribus et gallinis appreciatis vj*li*. xviij*s*. x*d*. ob.

Inde dimissa ad firmam per [? senescallum] die lune proximo ante festum Sancti Vincenti anno xxvj^{to} Regis nunc usque ad finem vj annorum[1] proxime sequentium et plenarie completorum, videlicet,

De [? Thoma de Y]hurst pro j domo cum curtilagio de tenemento quondam Johannis Thes per annum ij*s*.

De Willelmo [? Col]cok pro ~~iiij~~ v acris terre de eodem tenemento iiij*s*. per annum.

[1] This word is not very clear, but can hardly be anything but annorum. The bailiff, it will be seen, granted leases for one year, and these must be longer terms granted by the steward.

De eodem Willelmo pro ij curtilagiis quondam Dusebard et Furselonde per annum xij*d*.

Verte aliam partem

[Dorse] De Johanne [Raunde] pro j acra terre quondam Willelmi atte Strete x*d*. per annum.

De Thoma Poteflode pro j curtilagio ij acris et dimidia terre de eodem tenemento iij*s*. per annum.

De eodem Thoma pro j curtilagio et dimidia acra terre quondam Willelmi Hugon j crofto et iij acris terre quondam Simonis in the Lane et j acra terre quondam Daubereslonde vij*s*.

De Vicario de Banstede pro j curtilagio j acra et iij rodis terre quondam Simonis Bode per annum iiij*s*.

De Willelmo Goderd pro j acra terre quondam Thome Cole et j acra terre quondam Radulphi filii Vicarii per annum ij*s*. viij*d*.

De Johanne Teg pro j ferthinglond vocato Edelotelond per annum ij*s*.

Et de eodem Johanne pro j acra terre quondam Willelmi atte Strete per annum xij*d*.

De Johanne Godesone pro j domo et curtilagio et dimidia acra terre quondam Willelmi H[ugon ?] et j virgata terre quondam Johannis Longe per annum viij*s*.

De Gilberto atte Pende pro j tenemento et j ferthinglond quondam Alicie Boytone per annum ij*s*.

De Johanne Chuk pro j curtilagio et dimidia acra terre vocata Vydelond et pro iiij acris terre quondam Thome Cole et pro iij rodis terre quondam Dungehulle per annum vij*s*.

De Petro Kinge pro j domo et curtilagio quondam Galfridi Cole cum hayghlelonde et pro j curtilagio quondam Ricardi Godard et j [crofto] quondam Radulphi Vicarii per annum xij*s*.

De Willelmo Shepherde pro j curtilagio et hayghlond quondam Dunghille per annum v*s*.

De Laurencio Kinge pro j acra et dimidia terre quondam Galfridi Cole per annum xviij*d*.

Et residuum omnium terrarum et tenementorum predictorum sunt in manu domine pro defectu heredum et firmariorum.

Item idem Ballivus dimisit a festo Sancti Michaelis anno xxvij^{o} ad terminum unius anni terras et tenementa subscripta, videlicet,

De Gilberto atte Pende pro j acra terre de terra quondam Simonis Bode per annum viij*d*.

De Thoma Poteflode pro ij acris terre de tenemento Godardi Thurston per annum ij*s*.

De [Johanne] Bryt' pro j domo et curtilagio quondam Willelmi Cole per annum iij*s*.

De [Petro] in the Lane pro iij acris terre de tenemento predicti Cole per annum iij*s*.

De [Radulpho] Lamput pro ij acris terre de tenemento quondam Dungehulle per annum ij*s*.

De Johanne de Bures pro gardino et le hayghlonde quondam Godardi Thurston per annum ij*s*.

De Willelmo atte Mere pro le hayghlonde quondam [? Videhaghe] per annum xx*d*.

Summa omnium exituum predictorum hoc anno iiij*li*. ij*s*. iiij*d*.

(At the foot of the schedule appears the note

Decasus reddituum de Banstede retornati in Scaccarium Regine per Johannem de . . .)

IV

THE BANSTEAD COURT ROLL

Mem. 6

27 October 1393

[Banstede]. Curia cum visu tenta ibidem die lune in vigilia Apostolorum Simonis et Jude anno regni Regis Ricardi secundi decimo septimo.

Essonia. Johannes atte Potte de communi per Willelmum Sanger j°.

Districtio. Adhuc preceptum distringere Willelmum Algar ad respondendum Willelmo Parker de placito debiti ut patet in curia precedente et bedellus respondet quod districtus fuit per unam patelam et unam ollam pretium iij*s*. que dictus Willelmus Parker habet in parte solucionis xj*s*. iiij*d*. Et adhuc preceptum est dicto bedello dictum Willelmum Algar distringere quousque se justificare voluerit.

Districtio[1] Adhuc preceptum est proclamare in foro et in ecclesia de uno multone et de uno hoggastro que proveniebant de extrahura in festo Rogacionum.

misericordia iij*d*. misericordia iii*d*. De Willelmo (iij*d*.) Charlewode pro defalta secte curie ideo in misericordia. De Roberto (iij*d*.) Sutton pro eodem ideo in misericordia.

Adhuc preceptum est distringere Johannem Lamput ad faciendum Monkis tenementum contra proximam sub pena xx*s*.

misericordia ij*d*. De Willelmo (ij*d*.) Hoke quia non presens versus Robertum Sutton in placito transgressionis ideo in misericordia.

[1] Evidently a careless repetition of the word above.

Willelmus Cole nativus domini dat domino de chivagio suo hoc anno vj*d*. ... vj*d*.

Ad hanc Curiam venit Thomas Popelot et cepit de domino per virgam unum tenementum vocatum Fretislond et est dimidia virgata terre et continet per estimacionem xij acras terre Item dictus Thomas cepit unum gardinum et continet quartam partem unius acre terre et dicta acra jacet juxta dictum gardinum habendum et tenendum totum ut supra sibi et [heredibus][1] suis reddendo inde annuatim v*s*. ad duos anni terminos viz. Pasche et [Sancti][1] Michaelis equis porcionibus et admissus est et fecit fidelitatem et dat domino de fine pro ingressu habendo iiij*d*.

finis iiij*d*.

Johannes Longeland decennarius ibidem presentat quod communis finis est pro capite j*d*. hoc anno iij*d*. Item presentat defaltam (iij*d*.) Willelmi Profyt (ij*d*.) Thome atte Combe.

Chalvedon finis iij*d*.

Johannes Clare decennarius ibidem presentat quod communis finis est hoc anno iiij*d*. Item presentat defaltam (iij*d*.) Philippi Wydenne Item presentat quod Johannes (ij*d*.) Clare j Henricus (iiij*d*.) ij Fuller sunt braciatores et vendiderunt contra assisam.

Walytone finis iiij*d*.

Johannes Waweer decennarius ibidem presentat quod communis finis est hoc anno viij*d*. Item presentat defaltam Ricardi (ij*d*.) Logger Ricardi atte Watere et Roberti Waweer. Item presentat quod Johannes (iiij*d*.) Whyte ij Ricardus (iiij*d*.) Legge ij Hawkyn (iiij*d*.) Gildyn ij Rogerus (iiij*d*.) Cok ij [sunt braciatores (?)].

Setelowmille finis viij*d*.

Johannes Coupere decennarius ibidem presentat quod communis finis est hoc anno j*d*. et non plus quia Johannes Janyn et Willelmus atte Coppidhulle fecerunt defaltam ideo preceptum est dictos etc[2] Contra proximam.

Coppidhulle finis j*d*.

Districtio contra proximam

Reginaldus Underwode decennarius ibidem presentat quod communis [finis][3] est hoc anno iij*d*. Item presentat defaltam (iij*d*.) Galfridi Huwet

Horlee finis iij*d*.

Walterus Dokisherst decennarius ibidem presentat quod communis finis est hoc anno ix*d*. Item presentat defaltam Willelmi (ii*d*.) atte Hoke. Item presentat quod Willelmus (ij*d*.) atte Hoke j Ricardus (ij*d*.) atte Watere j sunt braciatores et vendiderunt contra assisam.

Leyghe finis ix*d*.

Henricus Shipherde decennarius ibidem presentat quod com-

Tadeworthe

[1] Omitted in MS.

[2] i. e. distringere (see margin).

[3] Word dropped.

munis finis est hoc anno iij*d*. Et Adam Othyn ponitur in decenna et juratus et non solvit quia . . . [hole in document].

Decennarius ibidem finem v*d*.

Johannes Profyt decennarius ibidem presentat quod communis finis est hoc anno v*d*. Item presentat quod Johannes Leangre levavit sepem ad nocumentum patrie Ideo preceptum est prosternere citra proximam curiam et predictus Johannes in misericordia iij*d*.

Banstede finem xi*d*.

Thomas Coke decennarius ibidem presentat quod communis finis est hoc anno xj*d*. Item Henricus Clerc dat domino pro chivagio suo vij*d*. Item Johannes Feuterer Johannes Reynold ponuntur in decenna et jurati et non solvunt quia positi.[1]

Secundus decennarius ibidem

Thomas Popelot decennarius presentat quod communis finis est hoc anno viij*d*.

tercius decennarius

Johannes Tegge presentat quod communis finis est hoc anno ij*d*.

quartus decennarius

Thomas Brugge presentat quod communis finis est hoc anno iiij*d*.

quintus decennarius

Ricardus in the lane presentat quod communis finis est hoc anno v*d*.

sextus decennarius

Arnaldus Lovelane presentat quod communis finis est hoc anno viij*d*.

Item Thomas Parker juratus in decenna et Johannes Whyte similiter.

Hyda

Rogerus Hopper decennarius presentat quod communis finis est hoc anno ij*d*.

Hulle

Rogerus atte Hulle decennarius presentat quod communis finis est hoc anno iiij*d*.

xij jurati

juratus juratus juratus
Rogerus atte Hulle Johannes Fronke Johannes Feuterel
juratus juratus juratus
Johannes Lamput senior Johannes Clerc Ricardus atte Hyde
juratus juratus juratus
Rogerus Brustowe Ricardus in the lane Johannes Kyng carpenter
juratus juratus juratus
Thomas Popelot Willelmus Sanghurst et Thomas Bruggere presentant quod ij pullani provenerunt de extrahura ad festum assumpcionis beate Marie ideo preceptum est proclamare Item j multo provenit de extrahura eodem tempore ideo etc. Item presentant quod Thomas Berwe faceret clausturam inter communiam et terram de Rorwe ideo preceptum est emendari.

iii*d*.

Johannes atte Mere bedellus habet iij*d*. de recuperatione iij*s*. contra Willelmum Algar

Ricardus atte Watere dat domino de fine pro secta sua relaxanda usque festum sancti Michaelis vij*d*.

Baldewynus Covert pro eodem ij*s*.

[1] nō sol' q' po'.

Pirinella Lechesforde pro eodem xij*d*.
Cecilia Poteblode pro eodem iiij*d*.
Johannes Prest pro eodem iiij*d*.
Willelmus Westebeche pro eodem xij*d*.
Ricardus atte Hyde pro eodem vij*d*.

Ad hanc curiam venit Johannes Rande et sursumreddit in manus domini unum cotagium cum pertinenciis et postea dominus concessit dictum cotagium Johanni Rande et Thome Popelot habendum et tenendum dictum cotagium dicto Johanni et Thome et eis (?)[1] reddendo et faciendo redditus servicia et consuetudines Et fecerunt fidelitatem et dant domino de fine pro ingressu habendo xij*d*. — finis xii*d*.

Districtio

Homagium presentat quod domus et grangia Johannis Kyng in the lane est ruinosa ideo preceptum est emendare contra proximam Item presentat quod Thomas [Tyler] est etatis xij annorum et amplius et abilis ad recipiendam terram suam quia Ricardus Tyler pater suus non est compos mentis.

Diem

Johannes Hereward habet diem ad ostendendum copiam suam de dimidia acra terre contra proximam . . .

. . . cio Bedellorum[2]

Johannes atte Mere et Thomas atte Mere et dominus elexit unum illorum secundum consuetudinem manerii videlicet Johannem atte Mere.

Ad hanc curiam venit Johannes Lamput et cepit de domino unam virgatam terre quondam Johannis Longe ad terminum decem annorum reddendo inde annuatim servicia redditus et consuetudines pro termino predicto Et predictus Johannes sustentabit dictum tenementum bene et competens durante termino predicto et dat domino de fine pro ingressu habendo vij*d*. Et ad hoc invenit plegios Johannem Colcok et Johannem . . .

De accidentibus[3] ut patet in extractis

Afferatores { Johannes Burys, Johannes atte Mere, Johannes Colkoc } jurati Summa istius curie xxv*s*. vj*d*.

27 September 1412

Mem. 12.

Curia cum visu tenta apud Banstede die Martis proximo ante

[1] Unintelligible.

[2] The MS. is torn so that only part of eleccio remains. In front of 'Johannes atte Mere' is an erasure.

[3] acc or att in MS. which evidently stands for accidentibus (casual receipts). On the roll of 7 Rich. II is 'De acc ut patet in extractis xvjd', and in a Court of 17 Richd. II 'De ex amerciamentis ut patet in extractis'. Cf. Carshalton Court Rolls, 1392 (Surrey Record Society, p. 34) where accidentibus should no doubt be read.

festum Sancti Michaelis anno regni Regis Henrici quarti post conquestum tercio decimo.

Essonia — Johanna Charlewode Johannes Lompyt senior Johannes Wyker } de communi per Walterum Lagge

ij*d*. — Johannes[ij*d*.] Taillour quia non warantizavit essonia curie precedentis ideo remanet in misericordia.

districtio — Cum preceptum fuit bedello quod distringeret tenentes manerii de Chalvedon [ad satisfaciendum domino de pluribus defaltis secte curie][1] modo respondet quod districti sunt per unam equam et respondetur preceptum est [melius][2] distringere citra proximam.

cape magnum — Thomas Hydman optulit se versus Elianoram Hopper in placito terre et predicta Elianora sommonita fuit et non venit ideo cape magnum in manus domini citra proximam.

ij*d*. — Thomas[ij*d*.] Berwe ponit se in misericordia pro pluribus defaltis secte curie ideo remanet in misericordia.

vj*s*. viij*d*. — Robertus[vj*s*. viij*d*.] atte Mere nativus domini et totum homagium nativum quia non habent Willelmum Bode clericum Willelmum Bryghte et Johannem Bryghte nativos domini prout habent in precepto remanent in misericordia et preceptum est ipsos habere ad proximam curiam sub pena x*s*.

Johannes Huwet quia non reparavit tenementum suum vocatum Admondes remanet in misericordia et preceptum est illud reparare citra proximam curiam sub pena perdicionis ejusdem.

Homagium de Walda presentat omnia bene etc.

finis xij*d*. — Ad istam curiam venit Willelmus Whyte et sursumreddidit in manus domini unum messuagium et dimidiam virgatam terre cum pertinenciis in Banstede vocata Bodes ad opus Ade Taillour pro cujus sursumreddicione nichil accidit domino de herietto quia moratur tenens Et dominus inde seisivit predictum Adam habendum et tenendum sibi et heredibus suis secundum consuetudinem manerii per servicia inde debita et consueta Et dat domino de fine pro ingressu habendo xij*d*. per plegium Thome Popelot Et fecit domino fidelitatem.

finis vj*d*. — Ad istam curiam venit Johannes Tygge et sursumreddidit in manus domini unam acram terre jacentem apud le Whytlond ad opus Johannis Popelote Et dominus inde seisivit prefatum Johannem habendum et tenendum sibi et heredibus suis secundum consuetudinem manerii per servicia inde debita et consueta Et dat domino de fine pro ingressu habendo vj*d*. per plegium Thome Popelote Et fecit domino fidelitatem.

[1] These words inserted above line. [2] Inserted above line.

Cum homagium de Banstede habuit diem inter Thomam Coke querentem et Johannem Tygge defendentem utrum Alicia filia Ade Aldryche sursumreddidit [in manus domini][1] unum messuagium et duas acras terre continencia j ferthylong dimittenda se et heredes suos[2] secundum quod dictus Johannes in curia precedente allegavit modo homagium dicit quod nulla talis sursumreddicio facta fuit Ideo consideratum est quod predictus Thomas recuperet tenementum predictum Et predictus Johannes remanet in misericordia Et super hoc dominus inde seisivit predictum Thomam habendum et tenendum sibi et heredibus suis secundum consuetudinem manerii per servicia inde debita et consueta Et dat domino de fine pro ingressu habendo xvj*d.* per plegium Johannis Colcok Et fecit domino fidelitatem.

misericordia ij*d.*
finis xvj*d.*

Cum homagium habuit diem ad certificandum domino de quantitate dampni cujusdam subbosci subter parcum de Banstede per Johannem (xij*d.*) Gerard prostrati modo dicit quod est ad dampnum xij*d.* Ideo predictus Johannes remanet in misericordia.

xij*d.*

Adhuc homagium de Banstede habet diem ad certificandum domino de dimidia acra terre de superplusagio tenementi Thome Pays citra proximam curiam sub pena vj*s.* viij*d.* Et quia modo nichil certificant ideo preceptum levare vj*s.* viij*d.* de pena curie precedentis forisfacta.

vj*s.* viij*d.*

Homagium de Banstede presentat defaltam Johannis Taillour (ij*d.*) secte Curie custumalis.

misericordia ij*d.*

Item presentatum est quod Robertus atte (xl*d.*) Mere nativus domini ac bedellus manerii injunctus fuit [ex parte domini][1] per Robertum Odersale custodem parci ibidem cariare unum damum Londonam domino et illud recusavit et sprevit mandata domini ideo remanet in misericordia.

xl*d.*

Visus

Henricus Willi decennarius de Walyngton presentat ad hunc diem de Borghsilver per capita iiij*d.* Item presentat defaltam lete Willelmi (ij*d.*) atte Grene Ricardi (ij*d.*) atte Broke et Ricardi (ij*d.*) Buset ideo remanent in misericordia Item presentat quod Henricus (ij*d.*) Wylly brasiavit j et fregit assisam ideo remanet in misericordia.

Borghesilver iiij*d.*
misericordia viij*d.*

Willelmus Joye decennarius de Hyde presentat ad hunc diem de Borghsilver per capita iij*d.* Item presentat quod Johannes Hopper

iij*d.*

[1] Inserted above line. [2] So in MS.

mansit infra dominium per unum annum et amplius non positus in decenna et presens in curia et juratus est.

Borghsilver iiij*d.*

misericordia viij*d.*

Henricus Shepeherd decennarius de Thadeworthe presentat ad hunc diem de Borghsilver per capita iiij*d.* Item presentat defal-
ij*d.*
tam lete Walteri atte Lake ideo remanet in misericordia Item
ij*d.* iiij*d.*
presentat quod Johannes Hopper brasiavit j Johannes Hyller ij et
ij*d.*
Johannes Upton j et fregerunt assisam ideo remanent in misericordia.

x*d.*

Willelmus Kyng decennarius de Coppedhylle presentat ad hunc diem de Borghsilver per Capita x*d.* Item presentat quod Willelmus Calys mansit infra dominium per unum annum et amplius non positus in decena [et presens in curia et juratus est ideo remanet in misericordia][1] Et preceptum est distringere citra proximam curiam.

Borghsilver iiij*d.*

misericordia viij*d.*

Robertus Wawyer decennarius de Sydlomylle presentat ad hunc diem de Borghsilver per capita iiij*d.* Item presentat quod Johannes Grenyng mansit infra dominium per unum annum et amplius non positus in decena et presens in curia et juratus est Item presentat
ij*d.*
quod predictus Johannes est communis carnifex capiens lucrum excessivum ideo remanet in misericordia Item presentat[2] quod
iiij*d.* iiij*d.*
Ricardus atte Water brasiavit ij et Johannes Grenyng ij et fregerunt assisam ideo remanent in misericordia.

Borghsilver vij*d.*

misericordia xiiij*d.*

Johannes Roy decennarius de Lye presentat ad hunc diem de
ij*d.*
Borghsilver per capita vij*d.* Item presentat defaltam lete Rogeri
ij*d.* ij*d.* ij*d.*
Brystowe Willelmi Brystowe Johannis Bartelotte et Willelmi Hoker junioris[3] Item presentat quod Thomas Roy et Johannes Begote manserunt infra dominium per unum annum et amplius non positi in decena et presentes in curia et jurati sunt Item pre-
ij*d.* ij*d.*
sentat quod Willelmus Hoker senior brasiavit j et Johannes Begote j et fregerunt assisam ideo remanent in misericordia Item presentat quod Regia via apud Denehacche est submersa in defectu
ij*d.*
scuracionis fossati Isabelle Dene ideo remanet in misericordia.

Borghsilver j*d.*

Thomas Franke decennarius de Leangre presentat ad hunc diem de Borghsilver per Capita j*d.* Item presentat omnia alia bene.

Borghsilver vj*d.*

Johannes Tygge decennarius de Banstede presentat ad hunc diem de Borghsilver per Capita vj*d.* Item presentat omnia alia bene.

Ricardus Brugger decennarius ij presentat ad hunc diem de

[1] Struck out. [2] *presentat* inserted above the line.
[3] *junioris* inserted above the line.

Borghsilver per capita xiij*d.* Item presentat defaltam lete
ij*d.*
Johannis Taillour ideo remanet in misericordia.

xiij*d.*
misericordia ij*d.*

Johannes Whyte decennarius iij presentat ad hunc diem de Borghsilver per capita ix*d.* Item presentat quod omnia alia bene.

ix*d.*

Johannes Colcoke decennarius iiij presentat ad hunc diem de Borghsilver per Capita iiij*d.* Item presentat quod omnia alia bene.

Johannes Lompyt junior tastator servicie presentat quod Willel-
ij*d.* ij*d.* iiij*d.*
mus Joye brasiavit Arnoldus Lucays Walterus Brugger Johannes
x*d.* iiij*d.* ij*d.* ij*d.*
Herward Johannes Clerk Thomas atte Wode Johannes Taillour
ij*d.* iiij*d.* ij*d.*
Johannes Feuterelle Johannes Lomputte junior Johannes Colcok
ij*d.* ij*d.*
Arnoldus Lovelane et Petrus atte Mere ideo remanent in misericorda

[torn] iij*s.* ij*d.*

Ricardus Monday remotus est ab officio primi decennarii et adjungitur decene Johannis Tygge.

Arnoldus Lovelane	Thomas atte Wode
Johannes Kyng carpenter	Johannes Feuterell
Johannes Herward	Johannes Franke
Johannes Clerk	Henricus Blake
Thomas Hunte	Walterus Brugger
Rogerus atte Hulle	Willelmus Hoker senior

dicunt super sacramentum suum quod Regia via apud Sherwode
ij*d.*
strete est profunda per fodicionem Thome atte Wode ideo remanet
ij*d.*
in misericordia et quia Ricardus Brugger [decennarius ij][1] decennarius illud conc[elavit] remanet in misericordia.

iiij*d.*

Affuratores Johannes Lomputte junior Johannes Roy
Johannes Whyte j[unior]

Summa hujus curie cum visu xxxiij*s.* v*d.*

22 December 1414

Mem. 4.
Banstede

Curia tenta ibidem die Sabbati proximo ante festum Natalis domini anno regni regis Henrici quinti secundo.

Emma Feuterer Petrus atte Mere Thomas Popelote Johannes Lomputte junior Henricus Scoryer Rogerus Whyte per Johannem. . . .

Essonia

Adhuc preceptum est distringere tenentes manerii de Chalvedon ad satisfaciendum domino de pluribus defaltis secte curie citra proximam etc.

districtio

ij*d.*
Johannes Lomputte junior quia non reparavit tenementum

misericordia ij*d.*

[1] These words inserted above line.

suum vocatum Hugonestenement prout habuit in precepto ideo remanet in misericordia.

misericordia ijd.

ijd.
Alicia atte Coumbe quia non reparavit tenementum suum vocatum Tacles prout habuit in precepto remanet in misericordia.

misericordia vjs. viijd.

vjs. viijd.
Petrus atte Mere ac totum homagium nativum quia non habent Willelmum Bode clericum et alios nativos domini prout habent in precepto ideo ipsi in misericordia.

districtio

Adhuc preceptum est distringere Willelmum Hoker de Colley ad respondendum domino de transgressione facta in pastura domini cum ovibus suis citra proximam etc.

misericordie viijd.

districtio

Homagium de Walda presentat quod tenementum Nicholai Burstowe est ruinosum in defectu reparacionis ideo habet diem illud reparandi citra proximam Item presentant defaltam secte
ijd. ijd.
Curie tenencium terre Johannis Leccheforde Alicie Gaveler tenen-
ijd. ijd.
cium terre Johannis Hughwette Mabilie Prest ideo remanent in misericordia Item presentant quod Johannes Begot elongavit quendam[1] ovem matricem provenientem de extrahura prout patet in rotulo Curie sine licencia domini aut precepto domini ideo preceptum est Bedello quod distringat predictum Johannem ad respondendum domino de transgressione predicta citra proximam Curiam etc.

misericordia xijd.

xijd.
Homagium de Banstede quia nichil certificaverunt domino de quibusdam vastis et distruccionibus factis per Johannem Kyng carpentere in quodam tenemento quondam Laurencii Kyng prout habuerunt in precepto ideo remanent in misericordia.

districtio

Preceptum est distringere Johannem Bartlotte ad ostendendum domino qualiter ingressus in feodo domini videlicet in uno tenemento quondam Johannis Prest citra proximam etc.

misericordia xls.

xls.
Homagium de Banstede quia non elegerunt Bedellum set omnino eleccionem bedelli recusaverunt ideo remanent in misericordia.

misericordia xijd.

xijd.
Homagium nichil presentant ad hanc curiam de avisagio porcorum prout de jure debent secundum consuetudinem manerii ideo remanent in misericordia .

Homagium de Banstede presentant defaltam secte curie tenen-
ijd. ijd. ijd.
cium manerii de Chalvedon Ricardi Colcoke Johannis Lomputte
ijd. ijd.
senioris Willelmi Joy et Johannis Colcoke ideo quilibet eorum

[1] So in MS.

remanet in misericordia Item presentant quod Prior sancte Marie de Overee in Suthwerke ocupat quandam parcellam terre vocatam Colyneslonde quo titulo ignoratur ideo preceptum est Bedello quod distringat eum citra proximam curiam ad ostendendum domino qualiter ocupat terram predictam etc. — misericordia x*d*. districtio

Johannes Whyte de Banstede nomine Johannis Lomput
ij*d*.
junioris tastatoris cervisie ibidem presentat quod Johannis[1] Kyng
ij*d*. iiij*d*. iiij*d*.
junior brasiavit j Petrus atte Mere j Johannes Clerk [ij] Johannes
ij*d*. ij*d*.
Lomput junior ij Walterus Kyng j et Johannes Whyte de Banstede j et fregerunt assisam cervisie ideo quilibet eorum manet in misericordia. — misericordia xvj*d*.

Adhuc proclamacio facta est siquis calumpniare voluerit unum ferthynglonde quondam Ricardi atte Hyde in Dunshud' et nullus[2] apposuit clamium ideo remanet etc. — proclamacio

Preceptum est seisire optimum animal quod Johannes Leccheford habuit die quo obiit pertinens domino post mortem ejusdem Johannis citra proximam etc. — preceptum est seisire

Affuratores: Ricardus Bruggere, Walterus Kyng, Johannes Roy — Summa hujus curie li*s*. x*d*.

29 July 1433 — Mem. 11. d.

Curia ibidem tenta die mercurii proximo ante festum quod dicitur ad vincula anno regni regis Henrici sexti xj^mo^. — Banstede

Essonia:
Thomas Tegge per Thomam Popelote
Johannes Wulberwe per Thomam Leccheford
Walterus Bruggere per Johannem Lomput seniorem
Thomas Saleford per Johannem Wethemere
Johannes Frank per Johannem Clerk
Ricardus Bruggere per Walterum Kynge
Rogerus White per Johannem Colcok
Johannes Rychebele per Thomam atte Wode
Johannes Wowere per Johannem Bartlet

Johannes Scoryere optulit se in propria persona sua versus
ponit se
Johannem Seynesbury in placito transgressionis Et unde queritur quod predictus Johannes Seynesbury xx^o^ die Augusti anno regni regis nunc vij^o^ iij rodas frumenti ipsius Johannis Scoryere apud Stonylonde cum quinque equis destruxit consumpsit et — dies

[1] So in MS.
[2] Inserted above line.

conculcavit ad dampnum predicti Johannis Scoryere xiij*s.* iiij*d.* unde producit sectam Et postea partes predicte habent diem concordandi usque proximam etc Et predictus Johannes Seynesbury

ponit loco suo

ponit loco suo Johannem Wethemere versus prefatum Johannem Scoryere in placito predicto.

Homagium de Walda presentant defaltum secte Curie Johannis Arderne secte libere Ideo preceptum est distringere predictum Johannem essendi ad proximam ad satisfaciendum domino pro secta sua.

Et eo insuper quod predictum homagium habuerunt diem et in precepto ad certificandum Curie certitudinem loci et soli certorum terrarum et tenementorum jacentium in Lye que nuper fuerunt Thome Haytone modo existentium in manibus predicti Johannis Arderne et que quondam fuerunt Willelmi atte Lye que tenentur de isto manerio per cartam et pro redditu vj*s.* xj*d.* per annum qui aretro sunt per xvj annos modo presentant quod predicta terra vocatur le Southelonde et jacet in Lye inter regiam viam ducentem

districtio

de Lye usque Reygate ex parte boriali et terram vocatam Sketeslonde et Halecrofte ex parte australi et terram Willelmi Hokere vocatam Castellond ex parte orientali et j croftam Thome Stephene vocatam le Blakecrofte ex parte occidentali Ideo preceptum est bedello quod distringat prefatum Johannem in terra predicta vocata Southelonde pro redditu predicto contra proximam etc.

dies

Et preceptum est distringere prefatum Johannem Arderne pro fidelitate domino facienda pro omnibus illis terris et tenementis nuper perquisitis de Ricardo Herteswode uno feoffato Thome Haytone etc.

dies

Et adhuc omnes tenentes tam de Banstede quam de Walda qui racione tenure terrarum et tenementorum suorum tenentur per custumerium reparare grangiam domini apud Banstede et clausuram circa manerium ibidem habent[1] ad reparandum omnes defectus citra proximam sub pena etc.

misericordie iiij*d.*

Homagium de Banstede presentant defaltum secte Curie tenentium manerii (ij*d.*) de Chalvedone et Thome (ij*d.*) Berwe Ideo ipsi in misericordia.

misericordie vj*d.*

Petrus atte Mere tastator cervisie ibidem presentat quod idem ipse (ij*d.*) j braciavit Walterus (ij*d.*) Kynge j et Johannes (ij*d.*) Lomput j et fregerunt assisam cervisie Ideo ipsi in misericordia.

attachiamentum

Johannes Wethemere queritur versus Willelmum Bokyngham in placito transgressionis. Ideo preceptum est etc. ipsum Willelmum attachiare contra proximam sub pena etc.

[1] diem omitted.

Idem Johannes queritur versus prefatum Willelmum Bokyngham in alio placito transgressionis Ideo attachiatur ut supra ad respondendum predicto Johanni in placito predicto etc. — attachiamentum

affuratores Johannes Lomput junior, Petrus atte Mere } jurati Summa hujus Curie [blank]

21 October 1533 — M. 25

Banstede — Visus et Curia tenta ibidem xxj die Octobris anno regni Regis Henrici octavi vicesimo quinto.

Lye — Communis finis xiijd. — misericordia viijd.

Johannes Chasemore et decenarii ibidem venerunt et jurati presentant de communi fine xiijd. Et quod Johannes (ijd.) Somner Willelmus (ijd.) Nye Ricardus (ijd.) Mathewe et Thomas (ijd.) Petir sunt residentes ibidem et faciunt defaltum ad hunc visum. Et ideo remanent in misericordia quilibet eorum prout patet super ejus caput.

Sidlomylle — Communis finis vjd. misericordia vjd.

Johannes Staplerst decenarius ibidem venit et juratus presentat de communi fine ibidem vjd. Et quod Johannes (ijd.) Pollyne Thomas (ijd.) Wooer et Jacobus Calverley sunt residentes ibidem et faciunt defaltum et ideo remanent in misericordia etc.

Chaldone — communis finis viijd. — misericordia iiijd.

Johannes Nortone decenarius ibidem venit et juratus presentat de communi fine ibidem ad hunc diem viiijd. Et quod Johannes (ijd.) at Tye et Willelmus (ijd.) Turry servientes Thome Travers sunt residentes ibidem et faciunt defaltum Et ideo remanent in misericordia etc.

Wallyngtone — Communis Finis jd. — misericordia xvjd.

Thomas Nelsone decenarius ibidem venit et juratus presentat de communi Fine ibidem ad hunc diem jd. videlicet pro seipso Et quod Thomas (iiijd.) Hunt Cristoforus (iiijd.) Hunt. Robertus (iiijd.) Lacye et Henricus (iiijd.) Kebylle sunt residentes ibidem et faciunt defaultum ad hunc visum Et non solverunt communem Finem per eorum capita prout consueverunt Et ideo remanent in misericordia quilibet eorum prout patet super ejus caput.

Coppidhylle — communis Finis xijd.

Robertus Colcoke decenarius ibidem venit cum decena sua et juratus presentat de communi Fine ibidem ad hunc diem xijd. Et ulterius omnia ibidem bene.

Tadworthe — communis Finis xiiijd. — misericordia ijd.

Ricardus Richebelle decenarius ibidem venit cum decena sua et juratus presentat de communi Fine ibidem ad hunc diem xiiijd. Et quod Stephanus (ijd.) Gylys sunt residentes[1] ibidem et faciunt defaltum ad hunc visum Et ideo in misericordia etc.

[1] So in MS.

Banstede

communis Finis xiij*d.*

juratus in assisam

Johannes Tegge decenarius prime decene ibidem venit et juratus presentat de communi Fine ibidem ad hunc diem xiij*d.* Et ulterius omnia ibidem bene Thomas Puplett etatis xij annorum et amplius modo juratus est in assisam domini Regis.

Communis Finis xv*d.*

Ricardus Kynge decenarius secunde decene ibidem venit et juratus presentat de communi Fine xv*d.* Et ulterius omnia bene

communis Finis xij*d.*

misericordia iiij*d.*

Proclamacio extrahure

Ricardus White decenarius tercie decene ibidem venit et juratus presentat de communi Fine ibidem ad hunc diem xij*d.* Et quod Thomas [ij*d.*] Weller et Michaelle [ij*d.*] Lagge sunt residentes ibidem et faciunt defaltum. Et ideo remanent in misericordia Et unus aries coloris nigri precii [blank] in custodia Galfridi Richebelle provenit in dominium de extrahura ad festum Sancte Marie Magdalene ultimo preteritum Et proclamacio de eo facta est etc.

Tastator Servisie

misericordia iiij*d.*

Videlicet Nicholaus Jowerye venit et juratus presentat quod Thomas [ij*d.*] Kaker et Cornelius Johnson [ij*d.*] sunt communes Tipillarii servisie et Bere ibidem et fregerunt assisam Et ideo remanent in misericordia etc.

xij jurati

Extrahura forisfacta x*d.*

Proclamacio extrahure

Videlicet Thomas Kaker Constabularius Willelmus Richebelle senior Thomas Laurence Nicholaus Harwerde Thomas Stauntone Willelmus Smyth Galfridus Tegge Galfridus Richebelle Johannes Hylle Thomas Travers Robertus Couper Thomas Couper Johannes Hooker Willelmus Crust Johannes at Heth Willelmus Calverley et Thomas Chylmede jurati et onerati de et super diversis articulis hujus visus affirmant omnia superius presentata etc Et ulterius presentant quod una ovis matrix coloris albi precii x*d.* ultra custodiam in custodia Thome Travers provenit in dominium de extrahura per annum et diem elapsos Et ideo adjudicatur domino forisfacta etc. Et quod ij arietes coloris albi precii [blank] in custodia dicti Thome Travers proveniunt in dominium de extrahura ad sesonam Pentecoste ultimo preteritam Et proclamacio de eis facta est etc. Et quod Alexander Charlewode permittit arbores et subboscos supercrescere viam Regiam in quadam venella vocata Denelane apud Sydlomylle in Walda ex parte boreali ejusdem venelle Et Willelmus Otwey similiter permittit arbores et subboscos supercrescere eandem viam videlicet ex australi parte ejusdem vie ad commune nocumentum Et habent diem succidendi et emendandi dictum nocumentum citra proximum visum sub pena quilibet eorum xl*d.* Et inhabitantes in tercia decena de Banstede habent diem citra festum Omnium Sanctorum proximo futurum exaltandi et emendandi viam Regiam in eadem decena modo existentem nimis profundam ad commune nocumentum sub pena xl*d*. Et inhabitantes in secunda decena ibidem habent eundem diem exaltandi et emendandi viam Regiam inter Portam Nicholai Harwerd et Frankes Dyche sub pena xl*d*.

Et elegerunt in officium decenarii de Tadworthe Thomam at Halle
Et elegerunt in officium decenarii de Sydlomylle Johannem Hethe
Et elegerunt in officium decenarii de Chaldone Johannem at Hethe
Et elegerunt in officium decenarii de Lye Christoforum Wooer
} qui jurati sunt in eisdem officiis

Summa hujus visus—xij*s*. iiij*d*.

Affuratores
Thomas Travers
Robertus Couper
Willelmus Richebelle senior
Thomas Laurence
} jurati

Modo de Curia

Willelmus Marshalle in misericordia quia ad ultimam Curiam essoniatus est et non venit ad warrantizandam eandem essoniam. — misericordia ij*d*.

Adhuc preceptum est distringere tenentes terrarum quondam Ricardi Arderne et Edwardum Merlande filium et heredem Nicholai Merlande et Robertum Hardynge filium et heredem Roberti Hardynge ad satisfaciendum domino de relevio et ad faciendum fidelitatem prout in diversis Curiis precedentibus Et preceptum est distingere Henricum Leccheforde gent' ad respondendum de diversis redditibus per ipsum per diversos annos elapsos retractis prout in precedente etc. } Districtio

Adhuc vij acre terre in Lye nuper Johannis Bartlott Et ij acre terre quondam Ricardi Potfelde remanent in manibus domini. — Terre remanentes

Ad hanc Curiam venerunt Johannes Dannett (viij*d*.) miles Ricardus (viij*d*.) Covertt armiger Robertus Trappis (viij*d*.) jure uxoris Willelmus Hardynge (viij*d*.) Antonius Hardynge (viij*d*.) Henricus Burtone (viij*d*.) gent' Elizabethe Hawkyns (viij*d*.) vidua Johanna Maior (viij*d*.) vidua Johannes Russell (viij*d*.) gent' et Ricardus (viij*d*.) Alyngham de Nutfelde tenentes et sectatores hujus Curie Et petunt se admitti ad finem pro secta sua Curie hoc anno excusanda et admittuntur prout patet etc. } Fines pro secta Curie—vj*s*. viij*d*.

Homagium ibidem videlicet Ricardus Kelyke Willelmus Richebelle senior Willelmus Hille Thomas Laurence Thomas Kaker Thomas Stauntone Ricardus White Johannes Tegge Nicholaus misericordia xx*d.*

Harwerd Ricardus Kynge Johannes Hille Ricardus Blake Johannes Hoker Robertus Couper Thomas Thomas[1] Couper Johannes Burstowe Johannes Shoo Willelmus Crust Robertus Burstowe
iiij*d.* iiij*d.*
jurati presentant quod Edwardus Merland gent' tenentes terrarum
iiij*d.* ij*d.*
Ricardi Arderne Henricus Lecheford gent' Willelmus Marshall
ij*d.* ij*d.* ij*d.*
Willelmus Richebelle junior Margareta Burstowe vidua Ricardus
ij*d.*
Kelyk de Horley tenentes terrarum vocatarum Stombelhole sunt sectatores Curie ibidem et faciunt defaltum secte Et ideo remanent in misericordia quilibet eorum prout patet super ejus caput

misericordia vs. iiij*d.*

xx*d.*
Item presentant quod Johannes Kempsale firmarius de Kyngswode
xij*d.*
et Ricardus Lystney injuste occupant et superonerant communiam Domine Regine vocatam le Banstede hethe ovibus et aliis averiis
xx*d.*
suis Et ideo remanent in misericordia Et quod [blank] Chartam' de Codyngtone injuste succidit et prostravit j carectatam de Firsshys super communiam de Banstede Downe Et quidam
xij*d.*
Willelmus Felt de Chayham dictam carectatam de Firshis injuste cepit et abduxit sine aliqua licencia in prejudicium tam Domine Regine quam tenencium ibidem. Et ideo remanent in misericordia quilibet eorum prout patet super ejus caput.

Residuum hujus curie in dorso

obitus Johannis Lamberd

Conjunctus status

Item presentant quod Johannes Lamberd qui de domina Regina tenuit per Copiam Curie secundum consuetudinem manerii conjunctim cum Johanna uxore sua sibi et heredibus ipsius Johannis unum messuagium ac certas terras et tenementa in Banstede per redditum [blank] per annum Quarum quidem messuagii terrarum et tenementorum habuit unam medietatem sibi et prefate Johanne uxori sue et heredibus ipsius Johannis ex sursumreddicione Willelmi Muschampe et Elizabethe uxoris sue et alteram medietatem inde habuit in forma predicta ex sursumreddicione Willelmi Warham' gent' Et ij acras terre et dimidiam jacentes in Kendelhawe unam acram terre jacentem in Crochelande ac unam acram terre jacentem super Rydonhylle unam acram et dimidiam terre jacentes inter Wodmerstorne feld et Edwardes Croft Necnon unam parcellam terre vocatam Longhawe et little (?) Rydon' continentem circiter iiij acras terre Et unam acram et j rodam terre unde predicta acra vocata Stonyacre jacet in quodam Campo vocato Stonyfeld ac dicta roda jacet in quodam furlongo vocato le

[1] So in MS.

Sole ac eciam ij acras terre insimiliter jacentes in Clauso nuper dicti Johannis vocato Sevyn' acre quondam Thome Tayllour per redditum [blank] per annum Obiit post ultimam Curiam de tali statu seisitus Et predicta Johanna ipsum supervixit et se tenet intus per jus accrescendi pro termino vite sue Et quod Reversio omnium premissorum immediate post mortem dicte Johanne totaliter spectat Rogero Lamberd filio juniori et heredi secundum consuetudinem manerii predictorum Johannis Lamberd et Johanne Et predicta Johanna modo presens in Curia fecit inde domine Fidelitatem

Fidelitas

Item presentant quod predictus Johannes Lamberd qui de domina Regina tenuit per Copiam Curie secundum consuetudinem manerii sibi et heredibus suis unam acram terre jacentem ad finem de Haccherslane juxta le Asshe ij acras terre insimiliter jacentes in Pytland j acram jacentem inter Edwardes Croft et viam Regiam ducentem versus Croydone et j acram vocatam Roseacre jacentem inter terram Johannis Hylle et terram Thome Puplett vocatam le Hegge Halffacre dimidiam acram jacentem in le Soole Shott ac unam acram in Whiteland juxta le downeholdene inter terram Elizabethe Merland ex utraque parte quondam Nicholai Harwerd necnon xj acras et iij rodas terre divisim jacentes in diversis particulis in Banstede in Communi Campo ibidem vocato le Aldehey que quondam fuerunt Ricardi Kynge et Johanne uxoris sue per redditum [blank] per annum Obiit post ultimam Curiam inde seisitus per cujus mortem accidit domine de herietto unus equus precii xx*s*. Et quod Rogerus Lamberd est filius junior et heres secundum consuetudinem manerii predicti Johannis et plene etatis Qui quidem Rogerus modo presens in Curia ex certis causis et consideracionibus Petit de premissis admissionem sibi ac Johanne Lamberd vidue matri sue et heredibus ipsius Rogeri per Curiam adhiberi Quibus quidem Rogero et Johanne conceditur inde per Curiam seisina habenda et tenenda eis et heredibus ipsius Rogeri secundum consuetudinem manerii per redditus et servicia inde debita et consueta Proviso semper quod predictus Rogerus non intromittat de aut in premissis durante vita predicte Johanne preter ad usum predicte Johanne Et sic admissi sunt inde Tenentes et fecerunt Fidelitatem Et dant domine de fine pro tali concessione sic inde habenda xl*d*.

Heriettum xx*s*.

Fidelitas

finis xl*d*.

Item presentant quod predictus Johannes Lamberd qui de domina Regina tenuit libere certas terras in Banstede vocatas Herroldes alias dictas Todyfelde quondam Alexandri Cherlewode per redditum iij*s*. per annum obiit post ultimam Curiam Et quod ipse ante mortem suam inde feoffavit inter alias terras et

Feoffementum

tenementa Johannem Skynner de Reggate juniorem gent' Ricardum Moys de Banstede gent' Ricardum Stauntone de Croydone Thomam Skete de Letherede Willelmum Huntly Ricardum Best juniorem et Willelmum Cawstene ad usum ipsius Johannis Lamberd et heredum suorum ac ad intencionem inde perimplendi ultimam voluntatem suam prout per cartam suam inde eis confectam gerentem datum xviij° die Junii anno domini videlicet MDXXXIIJ^{cio} anno regni Regis Henrici Octavi xxv^{to} voluit et declaravit quod Rogerus Lamberd junior filius suus haberet omnia premissa sibi heredibus et assignatis suis imperpetuum reddendo inde et de certis aliis terris specificatis in dicta voluntate annuatim Johanne Lamberd matri sue durante vita ejusdem Johanne quandam annuitatem xl*s*. per annum ac reddendo inde annuatim Thome Lamberd fratri dicti Johannis quandam annuitatem vj*s*. viij*d*. per annum durante vita ejusdem Thome prout in eadem ultima voluntate plenius patet Et predictus Rogerus modo presens in Curia fecit inde domine fidelitatem

Declaracio Voluntatis

Fidelitas

Ad hanc Curiam venit Galfridus Lamberd in propria persona sua Et in complementum et performacionem certarum convencionum inter Robertum Couper ex una parte et Johannem Lamberd patrem predicti Galfridi ex altera parte specificatarum in quibusdam indenturis inter prefatos Robertum et Johannem confectis gerentibus datum—die—anno regni regis Henrici viij xxiiij^{to} sursum reddidit in manus domine Regine omnia terras et tenementa sua custumaria situata jacentia et existentia in parochia de Horley in Walda infra dominium de Banstede que predictus Johannes Lamberd nuper habuit ex sursum reddicione predicti Roberti Couper ad opus et usum ejusdem Roberti Couper et heredum suorum Et super hoc conceditur de premissis seisina prefato Roberto Couper habenda et tenenda sibi et heredibus et assignatis suis secundum consuetudinem manerii per redditus et servicia inde debita et consueta Et sic admissus est inde tenens et fecit fidelitatem. Et dat domine de Fine pro tali concessione sic inde habenda xx*d*.

Fidelitas

Finis xx*d*.

Ad hanc Curiam venit Nicholaus Harwerd in propria persona sua et per licenciam hujus Curie dedit concessit et secundum consuetudinem hujus manerii confirmavit Willelmo Huntly de Wodmerstorne et Thome Kaker de Banstede quandam annuitatem sive annualem redditum sex solidorum et octo denariorum exeuntem de omnibus terris et tenementis suis infra dominium de Banstede habendum et annuatim percipiendum dictam annuitatem sive annualem redditum vj*s*. viij*d*. prefatis Willelmo et Thome et assignatis suis pro termino vite Agnetis modo uxoris predicti

Concessio Annuitatis

Nicholai solomodo ad usum predicte Agnetis et assignatorum suorum pro termino vite sue ad iiij^or^ anni terminos videlicet ad festa Natalis domini Annunciacionis beate Marie Virginis Nativitatis Sancti Johannis Baptiste et Sancti Michaelis Archangeli per equales porciones annuatim solvendas cum clameo districcionis pro non solucione per xv dies Et predictus Nicholaus posuit prefatos Willelmum et Thomam in possessionem annuitatis sive annualis redditus predicti per solucionem unius denarii Et dat domine de Fine pro tali licencia habenda xij*d.* — Finis xij*d*

Injunctio posita et ordinata est quod nullus Tenens pasturabit seu conducet oves suas ultra quandam viam in communi campo de Banstede vocatam Croydone wey ante festum Omnium Sanctorum sub pena xl*d.*

Aceciam ordinatum est quod nullus conducet porcos sive porculos in communi campo de Banstede nisi ipsi porci sive porculi justificati sunt jugis et annulis licite sub pena pro quolibet porco tociens quociens aliter ibi venit ij*d.* — Pena pro Communi Campo

Datum est Curie intelligi quod Thomas Stauntone fecit incrochiamentum in communi campo vocato Coffadowne in earando et subvertando ibidem aretra sua[1] quandam peciam terre de solo domine continentem in latitudine dimidiam virgam terre et in longitudine [blank] perticatas in prejudicium domine etc.

Et eciam datur Curie intelligi per Ricardum Scoryar quod Ricardus Moys injuste fecit incrochiamentum super terram ipsius Ricardi Scoryer vocatam Magotte lande in erigendo et ponendo ibidem quandam sepem Et homagium habent diem supervidendi incrochiamenta predicta et veritatem inde dicendi et certificandi citra proximam Curiam

Summa hujus Curie——xxxix*s.* x*d.*

16 October 1581 — M. 23d

Bansted in Comitatu Surrie

Visus Franci plegii cum Curia Barona[2] tenta ibidem xvj^o^ die Octobris anno Regni Domine nostre Elizabethe Dei gratia Anglie Francie et Hibernie Regine fidei Defensoris etc. vicesimo tertio

Essonia

Thomas Mathew Jacobus Charleton Johannes Blake Thomas Colborow Willelmus Pitter Richardus Hoobart Henricus Birstow Henricus Simondes Thomas Smith Johannes Godderd Johannes Hooke Henricus Langley et Willelmus Michell essoniati sunt de communi

Rogerus Killick Constabularius ibidem juratus presentat omnia bene — Constabularius de Banstede

[1] So in MS. (for arando et subvertendo aratro suo).

[2] So in MS. The usual form on the roll, when not baron' is baronis.

Primus decenarius de Banstede	Averius Puplett { juratus presentat quod dat domino de certo ad hunc diem xij*d.* Sed tamen in misericordia ij*s.* quia decessit sine licentia et non revenit ad presentandum que ad ejus officium pertinet[1] licet solemniter exactus etc.
Secundus decenarius de Banstede	Willelmus Lusted juratus presentat quod dat domino de certo ad hunc diem xvij*d.* Et ulterius omnia bene
Tertius decenarius de Banstede	Edwardus Thorn juratus presentat quod dat domino de certo ad hunc diem xv*d.* et ulterius omnia bene
Tastator Cervitie de Banstede	Willelmus Kinge mortuus est
Constabularius de Tadworth	Willelmus Mathew juratus presentat omnia bene
Decenarius de Tadworth	Thomas Martir juratus presentat quod dat domino de certo ad hunc diem xviij*d.* et ulterius omnia bene
Decenarius de Chaldon	Nicholaus Richardson { in misericordia ij*s.* quia non habuit nomina residentium prout ei preceptum fuit et postea juratus presentat quod dat domino de certo ad hunc diem vj*d.* et ulterius omnia bene
Decenarius de Copthill	Johannes Puplett juratus presentat quod dat domino de certo ad hunc diem xvij*d.* et ulterius omnia bene
Decenarius de Leigh cum Dunshott	Johannes Codington juratus presentat quod dat domino de certo ad hunc diem viij*d.* et ulterius omnia bene
decenarius de Sidneimill[2]	Richardus Codington { in misericordia x*s.* quia non comparuit nec misit communem finem nec nomina residentium ratione cujus non potuerunt vocari ad serviendum domine Regine etc.
	Henricus Gander excusatus causa senectutis

m 24
Duodecim pro Domina Regina

Thomas Gawin	Jurati	Walterus Gawin	Jurati	Nicholaus Listney	Jurati
Thomas Wood		Robertus Cooper		Johannes Kerrell	
Willelmus Eaton		Henricus Woodman		Georgius Richbell	
Thomas Richbell		Willelmus Halle		Nicholaus Charington	
Richardus Browne					

qui quidem Juratores super sacramentum suum presentant prout sequitur videlicet In primis quod Johannes Washford Willelmus Bentley Nicholaus Gawin Nicholaus Charington Robertus Brown et Johannes Cooper sunt residentes infra hunc visum et sunt etatis xij annorum et amplius et adhuc non jurati sunt in assisam Domine Regine Ideo dies datus est eis et eorum quilibet[3] essendi hic ad proximam Curiam sub pena etc.

[1] So in MS. [2] So in MS. for Sidlowmill. [3] So in MS.

Item quod Richardus Puplett defecit cum carecta sua in reparacione viarum per unum diem et quod Georgius Richbell similiter defecit per duos dies contra formam statuti sed tamen quia Thomas Gawin ostendit rationabilem causam in eorum excusacionem Et super inde fideliter promisit et assumpsit quod predicti Richardus et Georgius intendent et complebunt predictos dies sic deficientes ante festum Sancti Andree Ideo respectuatur pena etc. ad quem diem si non perfecerint incurrant penam statuti

Item quod Richardus Bridger non persolvit suam partem sive portionem pecunie pro reparacione ponti vocati Plansford Bridge[1] sicut ordinatum fuit ad ultimam Curiam Ideo forisfecit penam tunc ei impositam videlicet xl*s*.

Pena xl*s*. forisfacta

Ubi ad ultimum visum etc Thomas Gawin super se assumpsit et promisit scrutare pro arcubus et sagittis secundum formam Statuti etc modo idem Thomas presentat quod in uno die comparebant coram eo iiij^{xx} et iiij tenentes et residentes infra Bansted predictam qui habuerunt arcus et calamos secundum statutum et qui tunc defecerunt arcus etc. citra illud tempus eis contulerunt arcus etc

Willelmus Hall electus est constabularius de Bansted et juratus

Georgius Puplett electus est decenarius primus de Bansted et juratus

Johannes Snellinge electus est decenarius de Tadworth et juratus

Georgius Hall electus est Tastator Cervitie de Bansted sed quia abest Ideo mandatus quod veniet ad Thomam Gawin ad recipiendum sacramentum suum citra diem solis proximum sub pena v*s*.

Ceteri officiarii remanent

Electio officiariorum

Modo de Curia Baron'

Johannes Lambert	Jurati	Andreas Lambert	Jurati	Johannes Hill	Jurati
Alanus Woodman		Matheus White		Richardus Bridger	
Willelmus Smith		Henricus Hill		Christoferus Crust	
Johannes Killicke		Daniel Lambert		Robertus Bristowe	

Homagium ibidem

Qui quidem jurati super sacramentum suum presentant quod Johannes Skinner [vj*d*.] armiger et Georgius Covert [xij*d*.] armiger sunt liberi tenentes et sectatores huic Curie et ad hunc Diem fecerunt defaltum Et quod Allanus Colcott[2] [iiij*d*.] Thomas Turner [iiij*d*.] Edwardus Otwaye [ij*d*.] Henricus Birstowe [iiij*d*.] et Johannes Duke [iiij*d*.] fuit[2] custumarii

misericordia iij*s*.

[1] So in MS. for pontis vocati Flanchford Bridge.

[2] So in MS.

tenentes hujus manerii et fecerunt defaltum ad hunc diem Ideo quilibet eorum in misericordia prout patet super ejus caput

Item presentant quod Georgius Kinge disposuit fossatum quod erexit super terras dominicales hujus manerii ante diem sibi inde datum ad ultimam Curiam ea intentione quod esset imunis a pena ad tunc imposita Ideo ad hanc Curiam ordinatum est quod illud disponat et perimpleat fossatum sicut ab antiquo fuerit ante festum Natalis Domini sub pena forisfacture xlvj*s.* viij*d.*

Item presentant quod non possunt consentire pro materia de Normear Ideo petunt quod amplius ne onerentur cum ea

Elizabeth Shoo et Joanna Tidy filie et coheredes Johannis Shoo petunt quod clameum suum Irrotuletur etc pro una parcella terre vocata Vetheredge continente xij acras quam Johannes Shoo modo occupat Et quod predictus Johannes sommeatur[1] essendi hic ad proximam Curiam etc. Memorandum quod predictus Johannes Shoo per spatium x annorum non comparuit

finis iij*s.* iiij*d.* — Dominus concessit licentiam Thome Kakett dimittendi ad firmam omnia terras et tenementa sua custumaria a festo Sancti Michaelis Archangeli ultimo preterito usque et ad terminum decem annorum et dat domino de fine iij*s.* iiij*d.*

extrahura ij*s.* exigentium — Ubi ad ultimam curiam duo oves presentati fuerunt ut extrahure et in custodia Richardi Bridger et presentatum quod unus eorum clamatur per . . .[2] et ei deliberatus et alter eorum permansit infra istud [manerium][2] . . . unius anni et diei et proclamatum secundum legis exigentium Et . . . vendit' . . . .[2] Richardo pro ij*s.*

Ad hanc Curiam venerunt Andreas Lambert et W[illelmus] . . .[2] et recordati sunt quandam sursumreddicionem eis factam per quam Georgius P[uplett ?] tenens customarius hujus manerii sursumreddidit in manus domini omnia terras et tenementa sua customaria infra manerium predictum ea intentione quod dominus concedere dignaretur omnia premissa prefato Georgio et Marthe uxori sue et heredibus de eorum corporibus inter eos legitime procreatis et pro defectu talis exitus Remanere inde Rectis heredibus dicti Georgii unde accidit domino de herietto per spetialem petitionem nisi vj*d.* Quibus dominus manerii predicti per senescallum suum concessit inde seisinam Habendum et tenendum prefato Georgio et Marthe uxori ejus et heredibus eorum inter eos legitime procreatis et pro defectu talis exitus remanere inde rectis heredibus dicti Georgii ad voluntatem domini secundum consuetudinem manerii predicti per redditus consuetudines et servitia inde prius debita et de jure consueta Et dant domino de fine pro tali statu sic

[1] So in MS. [2] MS. damaged.

inde habendo vj*s*. viij*d*. fecerunt fidelitatem Et admissi sunt inde tenentes

Ad hanc Curiam dominus concessit extra manus suas cuidam Willelmo Richardson unam acram de solo vasto suo jacentem versus borealem finem de Burrough heath Habendum sibi et heredibus suis ad voluntatem domini secundum consuetudinem manerii predicti per redditum ij*d*. per annum ac omnia alia consuetudines ac servitia prout ceteri tenentes custumarii tenuerunt etc. et finis inde ei perdonatur et fecit fidelitatem Et admissus est inde Tenens.

V

THE TADWORTH COURT ROLL AND A RENTAL

1 June 1394

Tadworthe

Curia domini Roberti Wyndesore Prioris de Merton tenta ibidem primo die mensis Junii anno regni regis Ricardi secundi post conquestum xvij^{o} tempore fratris Willelmi Odiham cellerarii de Merton

Homagium

Ad hanc curiam testatum est per firmarium et alios quod Thomas Gillem fecit domino homagium ut sibi preceptum fuit ad proximam curiam ideo cessat processus

Dies

Adhuc Rogerus Wyke Johannes Lyhangre et Johannes Lucas habent diem ad faciendum domino homagium ut in curia proxima precedente etc. sub pena cujuslibet xl*d*. etc.

Attachiamentum Misericordie iiij*d*.

Johannes [ij*d*.] Profete senior ponit se pro transgressione cum porcis suis in pastura domini

Henricus [ij*d*.] at Lake ponit se pro transgressione cum porcis suis ut supra etc.

Remanet

Adhuc j acra terre et dimidia vocata Gattysacre quondam Ade Lucas remanet in manu domini

Finis xx*d*.

Ad istam curiam dominus concessit Johanni Lucas unam acram et dimidiam terre native quondam Ade Lucas habendum sibi et heredibus suis secundum consuetudinem manerii per servicia inde debita et consueta Et dat domino de fine pro ingressu habendo xx*d*. Et fecit fidelitatem Et habet seisinam etc.

Fidelitas

Finis vj*s*. viij*d*.

Ad istam curiam venit Johannes Kynge filius et heres Ade Kynge et petit admitti ad duo tenementa quondam dicti Ade quorum unum continet unum messuagium xij acras terre et aliud vj acras cum una crofta terre continente unam acram Et admissus est habendum sibi et heredibus suis secundum consuetudinem manerii per servicia inde debita etc. Et dat domino de fine pro

fidelitas

ingressu habendo vj*s*. viij*d*. Et fecerunt[1] fidelitatem Et habet seisinam etc.

Tallagium vj*s*

Omnes custumarii qui talliari debent quodlibet[2] anno ad voluntatem domini dant domino hoc anno vj*s*. Item presentant defaltam Willelmi (ij*d*.) Chuk Rogeri (ij*d*.) Wike ideo remanent in misericordia etc..

[preceptum-est] reducere

Item presentant quod Thomas Schepherd Laurencius Nichelot et Willelmus Othyn nativi domini sunt commorantes extra dominium domini ideo preceptum est ipsos reducere citra proximam sub pena xl*d*.

pena

Item presentant quod tenementum Johannis (iiij*d*.) atte Hulle non reparatur prout preceptum fuit ad proximam ideo remanet in misericordia Et preceptum est reparare dictum tenementum citra proximam sub pena x*s*. per plegium Henrici at Lake etc.

Heriettum j vacca precii viij*s*.

Finis iij*s*. iiij*d*. Fidelitas

Item presentant quod Thomas Prophete qui de domino tenuit in bondagio unum tenementum et dimidiam virgatam terre native continentem xlj acras terre obiit inde tenens domini post cujus mortem accidit domino de herietto una vacca precii viij*s*. Et modo dominus concessit dictum tenementum et dimidiam virgatam terre Johanni Prophete juniori habendum sibi et sequele sue secundum consuetudinem manerii per servicia inde debita etc. Et dat domino de fine pro ingressu habendo iij*s*. iiij*d*. Et fecit fidelitatem etc.

querela

judicium

ij*d*.

Adam Othyn queritur versus Johannem at Hulle in placito transgressionis de eo quod idem Johannes cum porcis suis clausum suum fregit et herbas ibidem cum dictis porcis consumpsit et conculcavit ad dampnum dicti Ade xl*s*. Et dictus Johannes presens in curia cognovit transgressionem predictam et petiit taxari Curia Et consideratum est quod predictus Adam recuperet dampna taxata a[3] viij*d*. Et preceptum est levare dictos denarios una cum dampnis taxatis etc ad opus dicti Ade Et pro transgressione predicta (ij*d*.) remanet in misericordia

Affuratores Johannes Prophete, Johannes West } Summa hujus curie xxvj*s*. ij*d*.

Roll 2, m 1

14 November 1462

Tadworthe

Curia tenta ibidem xiiij° die Novembris anno regni regis Edwardi quarti post conquestum Anglie secundo

Essonia

Johannes Puplet per Thomam Blake Johannes Wilcous per

[1] Error for fecit. [2] Error for quolibet. [3] Error for ad.

Henricum Hydeman Johannes Richebele per Johannem Mathewe Thomas Poplet per Johannem Mathewe

Adhuc preceptum est distringere in j acra terre vocata Blakeputacre et in j acra terre vocata Patacre ad ostendendum domino qualiter et quomodo tenentur citra proximam

Et preceptum est adhuc distringere Johannem Richebele Thomam Groffham tenentes terre et tenementi nuper Rogeri at Hille Willelmum Lucas et Thomam Poplet ad faciendum domino homagium et cetera servicia debita et consueta pro terris et tenementis suis que de domino tenent citra proximam

Et preceptum est adhuc distringere in ij acris terre de tenemento Thome Gyllean' nuper Johannis Joye ad ostendendum domino qualiter tenentur citra proximam

Adhuc homagium habent diem reducendo Adam Odyn Johannem Kynge et Nicholaum Johannem Petrum et alios filios predicti Johannis Kynge nativos domini citra proximam

Omnes custumarii qui talliari debent quolibet anno ad voluntatem domini dant domino de tallagio hoc anno viij*s*. Item presentat defaltam Ricardi [ij*d*.] Colcoke senioris Ricardi Colcoke [ij*d*.] junioris Thome [ij*d*.] Holme et Cristine [ij*d*.] Franke Ideo ipsi in misericordia. Item presentant quod tenementa Thome [iiij*d*.] Blake et Ricardi Colcoke [iiij*d*.] de Banstede sunt ruinosa Ideo ipsi in misericordia

Afferatores Thomas Blake, Henricus Hydeman } jurati

Rental of 1474[1]

Rentale ibidem de terris et tenementis liberis et custumalibus . . . die marcii anno regni regis Edwardi quarti post conquestum quartodecimo tempore Magistri Johannis Kyngestone Prioris de Mertone et domini Johannis Gysborne cellararii . . . infrascript' — Tadworth

Terre et tenementa libera

modo Johannes Lucas modo J. Marshall modo Willelmus Rychebele

Thomas Holme tenet capitale tenementum et septem acras terre quondam Willelmi atte Hacche et postea Thome atte Lee Reddendo inde annuatim terminis Pasche et Michaelis equaliter ij*s*. vj*d*. et sectam curie de tribus septimanis in tres septimanas } ij*s*. vj*d*. ad Roffense [iiij*d*.] — . . . Lucas

[1] If the missing day in March is before 4 March the year is 1475.

	Idem tenet capitale tenementum et unam virgatam terre quondam Rogeri Leangre et postea Thome atte Lee continentem xxiiij acras terre Reddendo inde per annum terminis predictis equaliter vij*s*. et sectam curie ut supra	vij*s*. ad Roffense [xiij*d*.]
modo J Rychbele	modo Johannes Rychebelle Johannes Groffam tenet de predicto tenemento quondam Willelmi atte Hacche xiij (?) acras terre quondam Willelmi atte Lotte Reddendo inde per annum terminis predictis iiij*s*. iiij*d*. Et [blank] de eodem tenemento quondam Willelmi Rychebell et postea Johannis Rychebell Reddendo inde per annum terminis predictis j*s*. et sectam etc	v*s*. iiij*d*. ad Roffense
modo J Rychbele	Isabella Ho . . . . de Sh . . gdon . . . . . . sex acras terre nuper Willelmi Upton unde ij acre jacent in . . . vocato longe acre inter terram domini Prioris ex parte boreali et terram Leangre ex parte australi et j acra [jacet in longe] acre ad occidentalem finem dictarum ij acrarum inter terram domini Prioris ex parte boreali et terram leangre ex parte australi et j [acra jacet] . . . . . inter terram Johannis Rychebele ex parte boreali et terram nuper Willelmi Lucas ex parte australi et [ij acre jacent] in le Estshotte inter terram domini Prioris ex partibus borealibus et australibus Reddendo inde per annum terminis predictis [blank].	
Thomas Puplet	Johannes Poplet tenet unum messuagium et dimidiam virgatam terre quondam Johannis Lucas et postea Willelmi Lucas Reddendo inde per annum terminis predictis vij*s*. et sectam curie ut supra	vij*s*. ad Roffense
. . . Puplet	Thomas Poplett tenet unum tenementum et ix acras terre vocate Coppley quondam Thome Kyngeswode postea Thome Poplet postea Thome Kynge et postea Johannis Poplet Reddendo inde per annum terminis predictis xvj*d*. et sectam	xvj*d*.
	Idem Thomas tenet unum tenementum et xx acras terre vocate Gilbert Prophetes Reddendo inde per annum terminis predictis ij*s*. viij*d*. et sectam curie	Ad Roffense
Ricardus Mathew	modo Willielmus Scorier alias Blake modo Thomas Blake Ricardus Mathew tenet ij acras terre jacentes ex australi parte de Cockesden Reddendo per annum terminis predictis ij*d*.	ij*d*.

Summa [blank]

Terre et tenementa custumalia

Ricardus Colcok

Ricardus Colcok junior tenet unum tenementum et unam virgatam terre native quondam Johannis Colcok postea Walteri Prophette et postea Johannis Hylle (?) Reddendo inde per annum iiijs. terminis Sancti Michaelis Natalis domini Pasche et Nativitatis sancti Johannis Baptiste et ad Natale domini ij gallos et ij gallinas et pro operibus relaxatis vj bus. et dimidium ordei et vj bus. et dimidium avene et in autumpno ij opera et sectam curie de tribus septimanis in tres septimanas et quolibet anno ad castrum Roffense xiiij*d*. et debet talliari quolibet anno ad voluntatem domini — iiij*s*. et alia servicia ut infra ad Roffense xiiij*d*.

modo Ricardus Puplett Johannes Puplet de Bansted

Johannes Popelet tenet unum tenementum et dimidiam virgatam terre continentem xij acras terre native quondam Willelmi Lucas et postea Gilberti Lehangre Reddendo inde per annum terminis predictis ij*s*. et ad Natale domini j gallum et j gallinam et pro operibus relaxatis iij bus. j pc. ordei et iij bus. j pc. avene et j opera[1] in autumpno et sectam curie de tribus in tres et quolibet anno ad castrum Roffense vij*d*. Et debet talliari quolibet anno ut supra — ij*s*. et alia servicia ut infra ad Roffense vij*d*.

Idem tenet unam placeam continentem j acram vocatam Scatesacre quondam Thome Leangre et postea Willelmi Lucas Reddendo per annum terminis predictis vij*d*. — vij*d*. ad Roffense

modo Johannes Mathew modo Nicholaus Matthewe

Willelmus Mathew tenet unum tenementum et j virgatam terre native continentem xxiiij acras terre quondam Willelmi Prophete postea Willelmi Relff (?) postea Thome Lehangre postea Johannis Mathew senioris et postea Johannis Mathew junioris Reddendo inde per annum iiij*s*. terminis predictis et ad Natale domini ij gallos et ij gallinas et pro operibus relaxatis vj bus. et dimidium ordei et sex bus. et dimidium avene et ij opera in autumpno et sectam curie de tribus in tres et quolibet anno ad castrum Roffense xiiij*d*. et debet talliari quolibet anno ut supra — iiij*s*. et aliis serviciis ut infra ad Roffense xiiij*d*.

Ricardus Mathew modo Johannes Mathew

[1] So in MS. and in following cases.

Idem Willelmus tenet j tenementum et dimidiam virgatam terre native vocatam Wyotes continentem xij acras terre quondam Henrici Hydeman postea Ranulphi Wyote et postea Johannis Mathew Reddendo inde per annum terminis predictis ij*s*. et ad Natale domini j gallum et j gallinam et iij bus. et j pc. ordei et iij bus. et j pec. avene et j opera in autumpno et sectam ut supra et quolibet anno ad castrum Roffense vij*d*. et debet talliari ut supra

ij*s*. et aliis serviciis ut infra ad Roffense vij*d*.

[marginal note illegible]

Ricardus Colcok senior tenet j tenementum et dimidiam virgatam terre native quondam Johannis Kyryell vocatam Nicholettes quondam Johannis Nicholett postea [blank] Kyppyng Reddendo inde per annum ij*s*. terminis predictis et ad Natale domini j gallum et j gallinam et iij bus. et j pc. ordei et iij bus. et j pc. avene et j opera in Autumpno et quolibet anno ad castrum Roffense vij*d*. et debet talliari ut supra

ij*s*. et alia servicia ut infra ad Roffense vij*d*.

[dorse]

Johannes Franke tenet j tenementum et j virgatam terre native vocatam Odyns continentem xij acras terre quondam Roberti Odyn postea Johannis Franke et postea Cristine Franke Reddendo inde per annum terminis predictis ij*s*. et ad Natale Domini j gallum et j gallinam et iij bus. et j pc. ordei et iij bus. et j pc. avene et sectam curie de tribus in tres et j opera in autumpno et quolibet anno ad castrum Roffense vij*d*. Et debet talliari quolibet anno ad voluntatem domini

.... Franke

Idem tenet j tenementum et iij acras terre quondam Ricardi Longe et j tenementum et iij acras terre quondam Johannis atte Mither et postea Cristine Franke Reddendo inde per annum terminis predictis vij*d*. et ad Natale domini medietatem j galli et j galline et j bus. dimidium et dimidiam peciatam ordei et j bus. et dimidium et dimidiam peciatam avene et dimidium operis in autumpno et sectam curie ut supra et quolibet anno ad castrum Roffense iij*d*. ob. Et debet talliari quolibet anno ut supra

vij*d*. et aliis serviciis ut infra

ad Roffense iij*d*. ob.

Idem tenet quandam domum cum curtillagio quondam Johannis atte Mither postea Johannis Prophete Reddendo inde per annum terminis predictis xij*d*. et de Morents redditum ij*d*.

xiiij*d*.

Idem tenet j acram terre et dimidiam quondam dicti Johannis atte Mither Reddendo inde per annum terminis predictis vj*d.*

vj*d.* ad Roffense

Ricardus Colcok

Ricardus Colcok junior tenet j tenementum et dimidiam virgatam terre native quondam Johannis le Kyng nativi domini vocatam Walsshes et postea Walteri le Kynge nativi domini Reddendo inde per annum terminis predictis ij*s.* j gallum et j gallinam iij bus. et j pc. ordei ij bus. et j pc. avene et j opera in autumpno et sectam curie ut supra Et quolibet anno ad castrum Roffense vij*d.* Et debet talliari ut supra

ij*s.* et alia servicia ut infra

ad Roffense vij*d.*

Idem Ricardus tenet j tenementum et viij acras terre quondam Cristine (?) atte Mere vocate Harwes postea Rogeri Hille et postea Johannis Hille Reddendo inde per annum terminis predictis xij*d.* et medietatem j galli et j galline et j bus. et dimidiam peciatam ordei j bus. et dimidiam peciatam avene et sectam curie ut supra et quolibet anno ad castrum Roffense iij*d.* ob. et dimidium operis in autumpno Et debet talliari ut supra

xij*d.* et alia servicia ut infra

ad Roffense iij*d.* ob.

modo Galfridus

Ricardus Potlode tenet unum tenementum et medietatem dimidie virgate terre native vocate Collers quondam Johannis Kynge postea . . . Coller et postea Petri Potlode Reddendo inde per annum terminis predictis xij*d.* et medietatem j galli et j galline j bus. et j pc. ordei j bus. et j pc. avene et dimidium operis in autumpno et sectam Curie ut supra et quolibet anno ad castrum Roffense iij*d.* ob. et debet talliari ut supra

xij*d.* et alia servicia ut infra

ad Roffense iij*d.* ob.

Idem Ricardus tenet j tenementum et duas dimidias virgatas terre quondam Rogeri Rede et Henrici Hamond (?) vocatas Shepherdes postea Johannis Colcok et postea . . . Potelode Reddendo per annum terminis predictis vij*s.* et iij gallos et iij gallinas et pro operibus relaxatis vj bus. et dimidium ordei et vj bus. et dimidium avene et ij opera in autumpno et sectam curie ut supra et quolibet anno ad castrum Roffense xiiij*d.* et debet talliari quolibet anno ut supra

vij*s.* et alia servicia ut infra

ad Roffense xiiij*d.*

Willelmus Blake

Thomas Blake alias Scoryer tenet j tenementum et quartam partem j virgate terre vocate Lyrcokes quondam Alicie Lyrcok postea Laurencii Weste Reddendo per annum terminis predictis xij*d*. et dimidiam partem j galli et j galline et dimidium operis in autumno j bus. et j pc. ordei j bus. et j pc. avene et sectam curie ut supra et ad castrum Roffense iij*d*. ob. et debet talliari ut supra

xij*d*. et alia servicia ut infra
ad Roffense iij*d*. ob.

Idem Thomas tenet j toftum nativum cum gardino adjacente quondam Walteri le Kynge postea Laurencii Weste Reddendo per annum pro omnibus vj*d*. Et solebat reddere vj opera in autumpno.

vj*d*.
ad Roffense iij*d*. ob.

modo Ricardus Tegge alias Potlode

Ricardus Potlode tenet quartam partem j virgate terre vocate Smythes quondam Henrici Shepherd Reddendo inde per annum terminis predictis ij*s*. j gallum et j gallinam pro omnibus premissis et quolibet anno ad castrum Roffense iij*d*. ob.

ij*s*. et alia servicia ut infra
ad Roffense iij*d*. ob.

Idem tenet j tenementum cum gardino et quartam partem virgate terre vocate Lyrcokes Reddendo per annum terminis predictis xij*d*.

xij*d*.
ad Roffense

Idem tenet j tenementum et medietatem dimidie virgate terre quondam Henrici Shepeherd nativi domini Reddendo per annum terminis predictis xij*d*. dimidium gallum et dimidiam gallinam j bus. et j pc. ordei j bus. et j pc. avene et dimidium operis in autumno et sectam curie ut supra Et ad castrum Roffense iij*d*. ob. et debet talliari ut supra.

xij*d*. et alia servicia ut infra
ad Roffense iij*d*. ob.

VI

THE PERROTTS COURT ROLL

16 January 1447

Perrotts in Com' Surr'

Essonia nulla.

Scilicet ad curiam tentam ibidem xvj^o^ die Januarii anno Regis Henrici sexti xxv^to^ DATUM fuit Curie intelligi quod Johanna nuper uxor Willelmi Joye que de domino tenuit in bondagio unum tenementum cum gardino et suis pertinenciis quod quondam fuit Gilberti de Kent obiit et inde accidit domino de herietto una vacca precii vj*s*. viij*d*. Et super hoc testatum fuit in curia predicta quod predicta Johanna ante mortem suam sursum reddidit in manus domini predictum tenementum cum gardino et suis pertinenciis per manus Thome Cherlewoode ad opus Willelmi Hampton et

Beatricis uxoris sue habendum et tenendum predictum tenementum cum gardino et suis pertinenciis prefatis Willelmo et Beatrici uxori sue heredibus et assignatis ipsius Beatricis ad voluntatem domini secundum consuetudinem manerii pro redditu v*s*. vj*d*. ob. per annum Et sic admissi sunt Et fecerunt domino fidelitatem etc.

5 January 1461

Essonia nulla.

Ad curiam tentam ibidem v^to^ die Januarii anno Regis Henrici vj^ti^ xxxix^o^ irrotulatur sic venit Willelmus Cherlewood dominus manerii predicti et testabatur quod Willelmus Hampton et Beatrix uxor ejus sola examinata coram domino sursum reddiderunt in manus domini unum tenementum cum gardino et diversis terris cum suis pertinenciis vocatum Gilbert de Kent in Bansted que nuper fuerunt Joanne Joye ad opus Thome Popelott habendum et tenendum predictum tenementum cum gardino et terris cum suis pertinenciis prefato Thome heredibus et assignatis suis ad voluntatem domini secundum consuetudinem manerii per redditum v*s*. vj*d*. ob. per annum Et dant[1] domino de Fine pro tali ingressu suo vj*s*. viij*d*. Et admissus est et fecit fidelitatem ET POSTEA in eadem curia venit idem Thomas Pupplott et sursum reddidit in manus domini predictum tenementum cum gardino et terris cum suis pertinenciis ad opus Johannis Poppelott et Johanne uxoris ejus habendum et tenendum prefatis Johanni et Johanne heredibus et assignatis ipsius Johanne ad voluntatem domini secundum consuetudinem manerii per redditum v*s*. vj*d*. ob. per annum Et dant domino de Fine pro tali ingressu habendo x*s*. Et admissi sunt et fecerunt fidelitatem etc.

{ Perrotts in Com' Surr'

2 November 1490

Ad curiam Johannis Cherlewood tentam ibidem die mercurii viz. secundo die Novembris Anno Regni Regis Henrici septimi 6°.[2]

{ Manerium de Perrotts in Com' Surr'

Essonia nulla.

Testatum est per ballivum domini quod Johannes Puplett de Bansted qui de domino tenuit unum messuagium cum pertinenciis cum gardino et diversis terris eidem mesuagio adjacentibus vocatum Gilbert de Kent in Bansted que nuper fuerunt Johanne Joye postea Willelmi Hampton et postea Thome Puplett diem suum clausit extremum Et quod Thomas Puplett de Bansted est ejus filius et heres propinquior et plene etatis qui presens in curia petit se admitti Cui dominus ex mera gratia et voluntate

[1] Error for dat.

[2] This Court is not preserved on the roll itself but on a paper dated

concessit prefato Thome Puplett et Margarete uxori ejus seisinam in terris et tenemento predictis habendam eis et heredibus ipsius Thome Puplett ad voluntatem domini secundum consuetudinem manerii per redditum et servicia inde debita et consueta Et dant domino de fine pro ingressu inde habendo vj*s*. viij*d*. et fecerunt domino fidelitatem et admissi sunt inde tenentes Et accidit domino de herietto post mortem predicti Johannis Puplett una vacca coloris ruby[1] precii vj*s*. viij*d*.

1603, containing also copies of the Courts of 1461, 1447 and 1551. At the end is the following note:

'Gilbert de Kent
Joane Joye held this land in bondage and surrend: it to
Will. Hampton and Beatrice his wife and to ye heires of ye said Beatr
Thos. Puplett
John Puplett entreth as heire without surrend:
—— here to come in some surrend: wch I have not but next
John Puplett surrendereth to
John Puplett and he to
Phillip Puplett now to be admytted by surrend: from his father Jo:'

At the back is what seems to be the draft of an entry on the roll which has been struck out.

[1] ? error for rubri.

Banstead. From Lambert

Domesday. Richard of Tonbridge held of Odo of Bayeux. Whole manor worth ~~10~~ £10 under Edw. Conf.; later 100 s.; now £8, Lambert I, 29-30

I.P.M. of Margaret countess of Kent, 1258.
I.P.M. Henry III, 23/16 (C. 132) Lambert II, 84-85

"Margaret held manor of Banstead of Roger de Mumbrey for 3 knights fees + the same Roger held of the king in chief; and ... ~~5 marks were held of the manor de redditu assise, and~~ of the manor are held de redditu assise 5 marks + ~~he~~ are held 2 carucates of land of the manor value 100 s. + the pasture, wood (bosci), etc are worth ~~2½ marks +~~ 2½ marks a year, + the garden ½ m. And they say John de Burg is nearer heir + he is of age.

[illegible], 32.	Receipts	Expenditure	Balance
[illegible]5-6	£82. 3. 9¼	£60. 12. 7¼	£ 21. 11. 2
[illegible]6-7	£ 75. 3. 9¼	£67. 18. 5½	£ 7. 5. 3¾

mexican from acct of Ralph of Sandwich stew. of the manor 1275-6, ~~from the~~ Ministers Accts in PRO general series $\frac{1010}{9}$; and from the Reeve 1276-7, Ministers Accts in PRO, general series $\frac{1010}{8}$), 33.

1276 principal receipts: fixed rents £14, corn sold £13, stock sold £26 (sheep £16, wool nearly £6), wood £7, perquisites of court £17. Prin expenditure purchase of stock £33 mostly for sheep, large purchase of corn £14 indicating crop failure.

33-34
1277 receipts fixed rents £14, corn sold £25, stock sold £18, wood £5, fines + perquisites of court £11, Largest expenditures corn bought £21; building £~~21~~ 32.

1, 37 prices seem to be about, or a little below average.

Lambert I, 42. Acct of Ralph of Sandwich. Rc of 40 s. rec'd from Camel + Kingesbir from vigil of St Andrew the Apostle (Nov 30) in the same year to the first of May next following in the same year.

Lambert, I, 47. Acct of Wm the Reeve. Rc of 100 s. relief on death of John de Bures[3] for

Lambert I, 50. Acct of Wm the Reeve. A deal
about tiling and shingling; also glass windows for hall; also, for whitewashing &
painting & colors bought for purpose the
rooms of our Lord the King, the Queen, &
the Knights.

Lambert, I, 53. Extent of manor in 1325.
Arable land of demesne 348 1/2 acres.
only 2 knights fees contr. to 3 when
Hubert acq. manor; expl. South Tadworth
to mon. Merton, north to Southwark.
Free tenants at Banstead, incl. Covert of Chaldon
List of tenants in Weald
Tenants in villenage at Banstead, 78
most ca. 1/2 virgate, 7, whole virgate.
virgates vary in size greatly. In Weald much larger
Lambert I, 62, n. 1, no trace of house in 1680, nor
prob. long before. In 1325 noted as expensive
to keep up.

one knight's fee. Note 3. Found on inquis. that he held all land of Burgh of the king in chief by knight service because manor of Banstead then in king's hands, & those lands worth £10 a year, & ought to pay 12 s. a year for castle guard for Rochester Castle. John his son & heir then 23 yrs old.

Lambert, I. 50 Acreage sown, according to previous acct was as follows:

			qrs.	bus
Wheat	.. 90 1/2 acres, yield		60	4
Rye	.. 9	" "	7	1
Barley	46	"	33 (~~46~~)	5
Vetches	18	" "	5	4
Bean	1/2	" "		3
Oats	78 1/2	"	58	3

Lambert, I, 49, note 2. Building prob. cons. of large central hall, with knight's room & other rooms at one end & royal chamber or chambers at the other, the kitchen being a little way off & connected to hall by covered way. Framework of walls timber, interstices ~~covered~~ filled with wattle & daub. Stone not handy & expensive, bricks little used at this date. Walls plastered inside & white washed, & in part painted. White wash much used the-

ERRATA IN VOLUME I

p. 10. Second line of last paragraph, add *of* before *Banstead*
p. 22. Line 9, for *Christopher* read *Cuthbert*
p. 25. Line 25, for *for whom* read *whose*
p. 59. Under atte Lane for i. 52 read p. 47
p. 69. Enese. See ii. 20
p. 87. Note 1, for p. 300 read p. 299. Also in fourth line from bottom for 5*s*. substitute 10*s*. (see Surrey Record Society's volume on Taxation Returns p. xi).
p. 141. Note 1, for *hole* read *pole*
p. 145. Note 3, for *Fenterel* read *Feuterel*
p. 153. Omit *built and*, and for pulled down by *the Buckles* read by *Lord Egmont*
p. 156. First line, Tipell' de Mede should be in inverted commas
p. 159. Note 2 line 7, omit *by the custom of the manor*
p. 189. Second paragraph, for *who* read *whose father*
p. 193. Note 1, for 1653 read 1629
p. 200. Notes should be numbered 1 and 2
p. 241. For *William* Lambert read *Willmot* Lambert
p. 272. Banstead Down. There should be a full stop after (1324)
p. 281. Line 35, for 1514 read 1504
p. 283. Last line but two, Dawbers should not be identified with Dosbard. See ii. 87
p. 302 (also 193). Wardons. See ii. 79
p. 340. Line 21, for *opeributem* read *operibus*
p. 356. Line 5, for *curtatores* read *curtatorum*
p. 365. Line 3, for *quas* read *quam*
p. 376. For *Hervet* read *Hewet*

I. SUBJECT INDEX

II. INDEX OF PERSONS

III. INDEX OF PLACES

PRINTED IN GREAT BRITAIN AT THE UNIVERSITY PRESS, OXFORD
BY JOHN JOHNSON, PRINTER TO THE UNIVERSITY